=Bosnia=

WHAT EVERY
AMERICAN SHOULD KNOW

—BOSNIA—

WHAT EVERY AMERICAN SHOULD KNOW

ARTHUR L. CLARK

BERKLEY BOOKS, NEW YORK

BOSNIA: WHAT EVERY AMERICAN SHOULD KNOW

A Berkley Book / published by arrangement with
the author

PRINTING HISTORY
Berkley edition / March 1996

The Putnam Berkley World Wide Web site address is
http://www.berkley.com

ISBN: 0-425-15538-2

BERKLEY®
Berkley Books are published by The Berkley Publishing Group,
200 Madison Avenue, New York, New York 10016.
BERKLEY and the "B" design
are trademarks belonging to Berkley Publishing Corporation.

PRINTED IN THE UNITED STATES OF AMERICA

10 9 8 7 6 5 4 3 2 1

To my sister
Sherry, whose love,
patience and support made it all possible

CONTENTS

CONTENTS

ACKNOWLEDGMENTS

This book would not have been possible but for the assistance and encouragement offered by dozens of people to whom I am deeply indebted. First, thanks to Natalee Rosenstein of Berkley Publishing, who had the courage to say yes to this book when so many others said no. Thanks also to Jill Dinneen, Casey Hampton, Karen Ravenel, Jacqueline Sach and Janet Saines of Berkley Publishing for their invaluable help. For assistance in research, I would like particularly to thank Sandra Levy of the Slavic language section of the University of Chicago library, and the en-

ACKNOWLEDGMENTS

tire staff of the reference section of the Oak Lawn Public Library. For help in preparing materials I would like to thank Tricia O'Connor, Helen Pula, Barbara Staskiewicz, and Marge Villalobos, who were indispensable. For reviewing the initial drafts and offering their suggestions, Matthew Blackledge, Ben Castiello, Mr. and Mrs. Scott Christensen, Mr. and Mrs. James Granowski, Fritz Heinzen, Richard Longworth, John Murphy, Joan Sherlock, Mike Sweeney, and Milan Vego were particularly helpful. Design and editorial suggestions came from Patricia Berger and Arthur Brown. Equally important to those professionals who helped bring this book to print are the members of my family who have endured the process and the author. I have been particularly blessed with the love and support of Bob Durst, Mr. and Mrs. Mike Francis, Leonard Sohmers, and Carol, Gloria, Keith, Kevin, John, Orval, Renee and Sherry Clark.

O tto von Bismarck,
when asked what would serve as a catalyst
for general war in Europe prior
to the start of World War I, replied:
"Some damn foolish thing in the Balkans."

=BOSNIA=

WHAT EVERY
AMERICAN SHOULD KNOW

PREFACE

The United States and its NATO allies have deployed 60,000 troops to Bosnia in the largest single military operation in the history of the alliance. Their mission is to implement the Dayton Peace Accords in the hope of ending four years of the most vicious war Europe has seen since the end of World War II. Their task will be both difficult and dangerous. In addition to deploying in the middle of the harsh Balkan winter, they will work amid millions of land mines, three hostile armies, tens of thousands of armed civilians, and numerous paramilitary and criminal groups. They will confront religious, ethnic, and political tensions that have simmered, and sometimes exploded violently, over hun-

PREFACE

dreds of years. They will have to deal with the physical destruction that has left a country in ruins, caused over 200,000 deaths, left more than 2 million people homeless, and caused tens of thousands to suffer torture and sexual abuse. They will attempt to implement an agreement brokered by the United States and signed by the presidents of Bosnia, Croatia, and Serbia. The agreement does not enjoy the enthusiastic support of any of the signatories, nor is it wholly acceptable to the thousands of individuals for whom these men speak. The agreement comes in the wake of numerous violations of previous cease-fires, several failed peace efforts, and tensions between the United States, its NATO allies, and Russia. The primary underlying factor that made this agreement possible is fear. Fear on the part of the parties that if the war continued it would be at even greater costs. Fear on the part of the United States, NATO, and other nations that if the war continued it was likely to spread to other countries in the region, as it has on four separate occasions in this century, with far more severe repercussions for both Europe and the world.

Because of these difficulties and the consequences should this agreement fail, numerous questions have arisen: How can one region spawn such turmoil and enmity? What must we know about the people of that region and their history if we are to respond intelligently to the difficulties that lie ahead? What are the details of

PREFACE

the peace accords? How will U.S. and NATO forces perform their mission? What military lessons should U.S. and NATO troops be mindful of?

This book attempts to answer these and other questions. It provides the reader with a brief historical overview of the Balkans and the wars that have taken place among and within the republics of the former Yugoslavia. The Balkan region is considered as a whole because the current turmoil in Bosnia-Herzegovina emerges from it inasmuch as the former Yugoslavia was essentially a microcosm of the competing national, ethnic, and religious forces that have governed the region. The book then discusses the remainder of the questions posed.

In a book of this size, it would be impossible to provide a detailed history of any single nation, let alone the entire region and the forces that have shaped it. The chapters do, however, provide a concise treatment of each subject, which should allow the reader to become familiar with the major themes of this conflict as the events of Operation Joint Endeavor unfold. Open historical and governmental sources as well as reports from the current media serve as the basis for the information presented. The maps and statistical information are derived from unclassified publications of the U.S. Congress, the Central Intelligence Agency, and the Department of Defense. No classified information is discussed; however, the most current unclassified information is presented. The reader

PREFACE

should also note that the views expressed are solely those of the author and that no governmental approval or disapproval of the information or views presented should be inferred.

CHAPTER 1

A CONCISE HISTORY OF THE BALKAN REGION

The Balkans (from the Turkish word for "mountains") comprise the countries of Albania, Bulgaria, Greece, Hungary, Romania, Turkey, and the states that have emerged from the former republic of Yugoslavia: Bosnia-Herzegovina, Croatia, Macedonia, Montenegro, Serbia, and Slovenia.

The Balkans' strategic position at the southern crossroads of Europe and Asia has been the source of the region's diversity and turmoil. With the exception of the Macedonian Empire, which emerged circa 400 B.C. and ended with Alexander the Great in 323 B.C., the region generally has formed the outer edge of other great and competing empires.

From approximately 323 B.C. until early in this century, the Balkan countries have been invaded, contested, and ruled successively or concurrently by the Roman, Byzantine, Slav, Bulgar, Venetian, Austro-Hungarian, and Ottoman empires. During this period of roughly 2,200 years, the peoples of the region have enjoyed important but short-lived periods of independence from domination by major empires.

The nations that emerged in this region possessed many of the features necessary for national development—for example, common language, religion, and ethnic heritage—but they failed to sustain themselves for three principal reasons. First, the mountainous terrain of the area made continuous central control difficult. Second, the proximity of competing national groups, who themselves had begun their own development, often brought these small states into conflict with one another in a contest for arable land. Resources devoted to these conflicts denied them the means and the time needed to sustain national development. Finally, most of these opportunistic states emerged during periods of weakness of a dominant empire. When internal or international circumstances permitted the dominant empire to reassert itself or to be supplanted by a stronger rival, these smaller states collapsed in the face of superior military power.

These periods of independence remain important in this region, however, because they provided the historical core from which the Balkan states began to reemerge in the mid-nineteenth century. These periods of independence also serve in part as justification for the competing, and sometimes mythical, territorial claims that are made today.

MODERN HISTORY

The present states and boundaries of the Balkans began to emerge in the mid-nineteenth century. Developments in the region were governed by two principal forces. The first was nationalism and the drive for democracy, with the former being more dominant; the second force was the competition that existed among the three major imperial powers—Britain, Austria (later Austro-Hungary), and Russia—for dominance of the area in the waning days of the Ottoman Empire.

The French Revolution triggered a reawakening of national consciousness on the part of many people in the Balkans. Nationalism—the drive for the formation of a nation-state by a people with common language, ethnic, and religious ties—spawned local uprisings, primarily against Ottoman control. Developments in Europe in technology, transportation, and communication made local resistance easier and sustainable, unlike earlier attempts. The Serbs rose up in 1813, the Greeks in 1821, and both eventually won independence. They were followed by the Rumanians, Bulgarians, Albanians, and Montenegrins, who first won autonomy and then outright independence. Similarly, Hungarians rose up against Austria, leading to the formation of the Austro-Hungarian monarchy in 1867.

The forces of nationalism were accelerated by both common and competing desires on the part of the imperial powers. Britain, Austria, and Russia, as Christian states, identified with the local populations' desire to be free of Ottoman Muslim control. This was particularly true for the Austro-Hungarian Empire (with the Roman Catholic populations of Hungary and Croatia) and the Russian Empire (with the Orthodox Christians of Romania, Bulgaria, Greece, and Serbia), who also wanted to be free of Ottoman control.* More importantly, this religious concern coincided with larger imperial territorial concerns. Before the emergence of a greater military threat in the form of a unified Germany, the British Empire sought to limit Russian expansion to the south and the west. Without such limits, the Russian Empire could advance directly into the Mediterranean as a rival naval power and eventually jeopardize India, Britain's prime possession in the East.

The Austrian Empire, and later Austro-Hungary, saw in the region an opportunity for expansion to the south at Ottoman expense and to the east into Romania. The Russian Empire saw in the area an opportunity for expansion, given not only its ethnic link to Slavic popula-

---

* Two exceptions are the Albanian and Muslim populations of Bosnia-Herzegovina who, although Muslim, were and remain essentially Western in thought and who, like their neighbors, sought to overthrow Ottoman political rule.

tions but also the bargaining value of the Balkans in dealing with its imperial rivals.

These larger ambitions resulted in various alliances during a hundred-year period from 1814 to 1914: (1) one or more imperial rivals allied against the other, (2) one or more imperial rivals allied against the Ottomans, (3) one or more imperial rivals allied with the Ottomans against another imperial state, (4) one or more Balkan states allied with one or more imperial states against the Ottomans, and (5) one or more Balkan states allied with each other against one or more other Balkan states.

This chaos resulted in several smaller, local wars during the period and served as a major cause of the outbreak of World War I in 1914. That war, the first one that was global in scope, resulted in the end of the Austro-Hungarian, German, Russian, and Ottoman empires and marked the solidification of the current borders of Albania, Bulgaria, Greece, Romania, Turkey, and the former republic of Yugoslavia.*

---

* World War II was marked by other border conflicts in the region, but current borders were reestablished after the war. Russian (then Soviet) influence reasserted itself and continued until the end of the Cold War in 1989.

CHAPTER 2

THE
BALKAN
STATES

ALBANIA

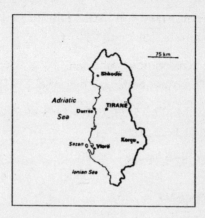

GEOGRAPHY

TOTAL AREA: 28,750 sq km

U.S. COMPARISON: Slightly larger than Maryland

BORDERING STATES: Greece, Macedonia, and Serbia-Montenegro (Yugoslavia)

GEOSTRATEGIC SIGNIFICANCE: Strategic location on Strait of Otranto, which links the Adriatic Sea to Ionian and Mediterranean seas

ALBANIA

POPULATION

TOTAL POPULATION: 3,413,904 (July 1995 est.); 1.16% growth rate (1995 est.)

ETHNIC COMPOSITION: Albanian, 95%; Greek, 3%; Vlach, Gypsy, Serb, and Bulgarian 2% (1989 est.)

RELIGION: Muslim, 70%; Greek Orthodox, 20%; Roman Catholic, 10%

LITERACY: 72% (1955)

GOVERNMENT

TYPE: Newly democratic

CAPITAL: Tiranë

PRESIDENT: Sali Berisha

PRIME MINISTER: Aleksander Meksi

SUFFRAGE: Universal and compulsory from age 18

ECONOMY

CURRENCY: Lek

GDP: $3.8 billion; per capita, $1,110; real growth rate, 11% (1994 est.)

INFLATION: 16% annually (1994 est.)

ALBANIA

UNEMPLOYMENT: 18% (1994 est.)

EXPORTS: $112 million (1993 est.)

INDUSTRIES: Food processing, textiles and clothing, lumber, oil, cement, chemicals, basic metals, and hydropower

AGRICULTURE: 4% of arable land used for wide range of crops and livestock; one-half of work force employed in farming

NOTE: Industrial growth rate, −10% (1993 est.). The nation is emerging from over 40 years of Stalinist-type rule with the lowest standard of living in Europe. Significant efforts are being made to move to a more market-oriented economy. This transition is likely to take a long time.

MILITARY

BRANCHES: Army, navy, air and air defense forces, Interior Ministry troops

MANPOWER AVAILABILITY: Males 15–49 years of age, 919,085; 755,574 fit for military service; 33,323 reach military age (19) annually (1995 est.)

ALBANIA

CURRENT DISPUTES

Concern over treatment of ethnic Albanians in Serbia and Macedonia; northern Epirus border question with Greece; concern over treatment of ethnic Albanian population in Greece

BULGARIA

GEOGRAPHY

TOTAL AREA: 110,910 sq km

U.S. COMPARISON: Slightly larger than Tennessee

BORDERING STATES: Greece, Macedonia, Romania, Serbia-Montenegro (Yugoslavia), and Turkey

GEOSTRATEGIC SIGNIFICANCE: Located near Turkish straits; controls key land routes from Europe to Middle East and Asia

BULGARIA

POPULATION

TOTAL POPULATION: 8,775,198 (July 1995 est.); −0.25% growth rate (1995 est.)

ETHNIC COMPOSITION: Bulgarian, 85.3%; Turk, 8.5%; Gypsy, 2.6%; Macedonian, 2.5%; Armenian, 0.3%; Russian, 0.2%; other, 0.6%

RELIGION: Bulgarian Orthodox, 85%; Muslim, 13%; Jewish, 0.8%; Roman Catholic, 0.5%; Uniate Catholic, 0.2%; Protestant, Gregorian-Armenian, and other, 0.5%

LITERACY: 98% (1992 est.)

GOVERNMENT

TYPE: Newly democratic with diminishing Communist Party influence in the countryside

CAPITAL: Sofia

PRESIDENT: Zhelyu Zhelev

PRIME MINISTER: Zhan Videnov

SUFFRAGE: Universal and compulsory from age 18

BULGARIA

ECONOMY

CURRENCY: Lev

GDP: $33.7 billion; per capita, $3,830; real growth rate, 0.2% (1994 est.)

INFLATION: 122% annually (1994 est.)

UNEMPLOYMENT: 16% (1994 est.)

EXPORTS: $3.6 billion (1993)

INDUSTRIES: Machine building and metalworking, food processing, chemicals, textiles, building materials, ferrous and nonferrous metals

AGRICULTURE: One-third of arable land devoted to growing grain; surplus food producer

NOTE: The country continues to make progress in its transformation from a planned and state-controlled economy to a market economy. Allows foreign investment.

MILITARY

BRANCHES: Army, navy, air and air defense forces, frontier troops, and internal defense troops

MANPOWER AVAILABILITY: Males 15–49 years of age,

BULGARIA

2,171,414; 1,810,989 fit for military service; 69,200 reach military age (19) annually (1995 est.)

ALLIANCES: Former member of Warsaw Pact

CURRENT DISPUTES

Macedonia question with Greece and Serbia

GREECE

GEOGRAPHY

TOTAL AREA: 131,940 sq km

U.S. COMPARISON: Slightly smaller than Alabama

BORDERING STATES: Albania, Bulgaria, Turkey, and Macedonia

GEOSTRATEGIC SIGNIFICANCE: Dominates Aegean Sea and southern approach to Turkish straits

GREECE

POPULATION

TOTAL POPULATION: 10,647,511 (July 1995 est.); 0.72% growth rate (1995 est.)

ETHNIC COMPOSITION: Greek, 98%; other, 2%

RELIGION: Greek Orthodox, 98%; Muslim, 1.3%; other, 0.7%

LITERACY: 95% (1991 est.)

GOVERNMENT

TYPE: Presidential parliamentary government

CAPITAL: Athens

PRESIDENT: Konstantinos Stephanopolus

PRIME MINISTER: Andreas Papandreou (in critical condition as of Dec. 1995 due to long-term illness)

SUFFRAGE: Universal and compulsory from age 18

ECONOMY

CURRENCY: Drachma

GDP: $93.7 billion; per capita, $8,870; real growth rate, 0.4% (1994 est.)

INFLATION: 10.9% annually (1994 est.)

GREECE

UNEMPLOYMENT: 10.1% (1994 est.)

EXPORTS: $9 billion (1993)

INDUSTRIES: Food and tobacco processing, textiles, chemicals, metal products, tourism, mining, and petroleum

AGRICULTURE: 8% of arable land devoted to agriculture; self-sufficient in food except meat, dairy products, and animal feed grains

NOTE: As a mixed capitalist and socialist economy, Greece secured financial assistance from the European Community with strict conditions for reduction of deficit and public employment, but significant steps in this direction have yet to be made.

MILITARY

BRANCHES: Army, navy, air force, national guard, and police

MANPOWER AVAILABILITY: Males 15–49 years of age, 2,676,152; 2,676,152 fit for military service; 75,857 reach military age (21) annually (1995 est.)

DEFENSE EXPENDITURES: 5.4% of GDP (1994)

ALLIANCES: Member of NATO

GREECE

CURRENT DISPUTES

Disputes with Turkey regarding airspace, continental shelf, and territorial waters; Cyprus question with Turkey; northern Epirus question with Albania; opposed international recognition of Macedonian independence

HUNGARY

GEOGRAPHY

TOTAL AREA: 93,030 sq km

U.S. COMPARISON: Slightly smaller than Indiana

BORDERING STATES: Austria, Slovak Republic, Slovenia, Romania, Croatia, Serbia-Montenegro (Yugoslavia), and Ukraine

GEOSTRATEGIC SIGNIFICANCE: Strategic location astride principal land routes between Western Europe and Balkan Peninsula and between Ukraine and Mediterranean basin

HUNGARY

POPULATION

TOTAL POPULATION: 10,318,838 (July 1995 est.); 0.02% growth rate (1995 est.)

ETHNIC COMPOSITION: Hungarian, 89.9%; Gypsy, 4%; German, 2.6%; Serb, 2%; Slovak, 0.8%; Rumanian 0.7%

RELIGION: Roman Catholic, 67.5%; Calvinist, 20%; Lutheran, 5%; atheist and other, 7.5%

LITERACY: 99% (1980)

GOVERNMENT

TYPE: Republic

CAPITAL: Budapest

PRESIDENT: Arpad Goncz

PRIME MINISTER: Gyula Horn

SUFFRAGE: Universal at age 18

HUNGARY

ECONOMY

CURRENCY: Forint

GDP: $58.8 billion; per capita, $5,700; real growth rate, 3% (1995 est.)

INFLATION: 21% annually (1994 est.)

UNEMPLOYMENT: 10.4% (1994)

EXPORTS: $10.3 billion (1994 est.)

INDUSTRIES: Mining, metallurgy, engineering industries, processed foods, textiles, chemicals, pharmaceuticals, trucks and buses

AGRICULTURE: 6.1% of arable land devoted to highly diverse food production employing 16% of workforce; self-sufficient

NOTE: Continues to move from a command to a market economy.

MILITARY

BRANCHES: Ground forces, air and air defense forces, border guards, and territorial defense

MANPOWER AVAILABILITY: Males 15–49 years of age,

HUNGARY

2,639,860; 2,105,632 fit for military service; 86,298 reach military age (18) annually (1995 est.)

ALLIANCES: Former member of Warsaw Pact; seeks admission to NATO

CURRENT DISPUTES

Large ethnic Hungarian population in Serbian province of Vojvodina

ROMANIA

GEOGRAPHY

TOTAL AREA: 237,500 sq km

U.S. COMPARISON: Slightly smaller than Oregon

BORDERING STATES: Bulgaria, Hungary, Moldavia, Serbia-Montenegro, and Ukraine

GEOSTRATEGIC SIGNIFICANCE: Controls most easily traversable land route between the Balkans, Moldova, and Ukraine

ROMANIA

POPULATION

TOTAL POPULATION: 23,198,330 (July 1995 est.); 0.09% growth rate (1995 est.)

ETHNIC COMPOSITION: Rumanian, 89.1%; Hungarian, 8.9%; German 0.4%; Ukrainian, Serb, Croat, Russian, Turkish, and Gypsy, 1.6%

RELIGION: Romanian Orthodox, 70%; Roman Catholic, 6%; Protestant, 6%; unaffiliated, 18%

LITERACY: 97% (1992)

GOVERNMENT

TYPE: Republic

CAPITAL: Bucharest

PRESIDENT: Ion Iliescu

PRIME MINISTER: Nicolae Vacaroiu

SUFFRAGE: Universal from age 18

ECONOMY

CURRENCY: Leu

GDP: $64.7 billion; per capita, $2,790; real growth rate, 3.4% (1994 est.)

ROMANIA

INFLATION: 64% annually (1994 est.)

UNEMPLOYMENT: 10.9% (December 1994 est.)

EXPORTS: $6 billion (1994 est.)

INDUSTRIES: Mining, timber, construction material, metallurgy, chemicals, machine building, food processing, and petroleum (exhausting current reserves)

AGRICULTURE: 3% of arable land in use, requiring 28% of labor force; major wheat and corn producer

NOTE: Government continues to move from command economy toward one allowing private ownership; economic progress remains slow.

MILITARY

BRANCHES: Army, navy, air and air defense forces, paramilitary forces, civil defense

MANPOWER AVAILABILITY: Males 15–49 years of age, 5,934,524; 5,002,287 fit for military service; 196,587 reach military age (20) annually (1995 est.)

DEFENSE EXPENDITURES: 3% of GDP (1994 est.)

ALLIANCES: Former member of Warsaw Pact

ROMANIA

CURRENT DISPUTES

None directly related to current wars. Access to Danube River means potential impact on U.N. trade sanctions against Yugoslavia

TURKEY

GEOGRAPHY

TOTAL AREA: 780,580 sq km

U.S. COMPARISON: Slightly larger than Texas

BORDERING STATES: Armenia, Azerbaijan, Bulgaria, Georgia, Greece, Iran, Iraq, and Syria

GEOSTRATEGIC SIGNIFICANCE: Controls Turkish straits (Bosporus, Sea of Marmara, Dardanelles), which link Black Sea to Aegean Sea

TURKEY

POPULATION

TOTAL POPULATION: 63,405,526 (July 1995 est.); 1.97% growth rate (1995 est.)

ETHNIC COMPOSITION: Turkish, 80%; Kurdish, 20%

RELIGION: Muslim (mostly Sunni), 99.8%; other (Christian and Jewish) 0.2%

LITERACY: 79% (1990 est.)

GOVERNMENT

TYPE: Republican parliamentary democracy

CAPITAL: Ankara

PRESIDENT: Suleyman Demirel

PRIME MINISTER: Tansu Ciller

SUFFRAGE: Universal from age 21

ECONOMY

CURRENCY: Turkish lira

GDP: $305.2 billion; per capita, $4,910; real growth rate, −5% (1994 est.)

INFLATION: 106% annually (1994)

TURKEY

UNEMPLOYMENT: 12.6% (1994 est.)

EXPORTS: $15.3 billion (1993)

INDUSTRIES: Textiles, food processing, mining, steel, petroleum, construction, lumber, and paper

AGRICULTURE: 4% of arable land used in crop production; self-sufficient most years

NOTE: Recent economic performance has fallen from strong growth of 1980s; industrial growth rate, 6.7% (1993 est.).

MILITARY

BRANCHES: Land forces, navy (including naval air and infantry), air force, coast guard, and gendarmerie

MANPOWER AVAILABILITY: Males 15–49 years of age, 16,519,152; 10,067,089 fit for military service; 625,476 reach military age (20) annually (1995 est.)

DEFENSE EXPENDITURES: $6.9 billion, 4.1% GDP (1993)

ALLIANCES: Member of NATO; major recipient of U.S. military aid

TURKEY

CURRENT DISPUTES

Disputes with Greece with regard to airspace, continental shelf, and territorial waters; Cyprus question; concern over treatment of ethnic Muslims in former Yugoslav republics

CHAPTER 3

A
CONCISE
HISTORY
OF THE
FORMER
REPUBLIC
OF
YUGOSLAVIA

S ix states have emerged so far from the breakup of the former Republic of Yugoslavia. They are Bosnia-Herzegovina, Croatia, Macedonia, Montenegro, Slovenia, and Serbia.* Before considering the

---

* Under the Dayton Peace Accords, the Republic of Bosnia will consist of a unified central government and the two ethnic republics within its borders: the Federation of Bosnia and the Bosnian Serb Republic. Further fragmentation remains a distinct possibility. Separatist elements are also active in the Serbian province of Kosovo. The results of the peace accords may exacerbate these tensions as well as tension within the Republic of Serbia and the Republic of Montenegro, which together form the new Yugoslav Republic. These issues are fraught with the risk of far greater violence than has so far been witnessed and hold the possibility of expanding the conflict within the region. These issues will be discussed in this and the following chapter.

The Balkan Region

The Former Yugoslavia—Ethnic Distribution

Yugoslavia 1914 to March 1992

violence that has characterized the dissolution, a brief look at the history of this country will be helpful.

YUGOSLAVIA, 1918–1990

After World War I, the victorious Allied powers, principally Britain and France, redrew the map of Europe, the Middle East, and much of Africa. The boundaries that emerged in Europe, in conjunction with other factors, helped sow the seeds of World War II. The new boundaries drawn in the Middle East and Africa also became a source of conflict in both regions. The most significant feature of these divisions was the establishment of borders that often failed to reflect ethnic or religious realities.

Yugoslavia is a prime example. First known as the Kingdom of the Serbs, Croats, and Slovenes, its very name called into question the long-term viability of the country as a single entity. Created through the merger of the independent kingdoms of Serbia and Montenegro together with former Austro-Hungarian territories, the nation consisted of peoples who spoke seven different languages, professed three major religious beliefs, and used two different alphabets—Roman and Cyrillic—although Arabic script also remained prevalent in Bosnia.

The country formally changed its name to the Kingdom of Yugoslavia (Land of the South Slavs) in 1929. While the name gave the appearance of a shared national vision, relations among the principal national groups remained uneasy. During the period between the wars, the country's politics drifted from a paralyzed parliamentary system to a dictatorship under King Alexander I, until his assassination by a Macedonian nationalist, and finally ended in an ineffective regency under King Peter.

During the years 1929 through 1941, the collapse of the nation was prevented only by the use of the Serbian-dominated army and by the undesirable prospect of union with the Fascist states that surrounded the country completely by 1940. When Hitler's armies invaded Yugoslavia in April 1941, Yugoslavia ceased to exist. Germany occupied a portion of the country outright and divided the rest between its Fascist allies—Bulgaria, Hungary, and Italy—and the puppet state of Croatia, which was under the control of Croatian Fascists known as the Ustashe. Each of these states was responsible for the extermination of tens of thousands of Serbs, Jews, and Gypsies from 1941 to 1944.

From 1941 to 1944, Yugoslavia suffered both from its attempts to fight Fascist occupation during the war and from an internal civil war among competing national and political factions for control of the country after the war. The multifaceted nature of the civil war characterizes in many ways the current conflict. Contestants were divided along both national lines (e.g., Serbs vs. Croats) and political lines (e.g., Serb republicans vs. Serb royalists; Yugoslav nationalists vs. Yugoslav Communist nationalists). The only common feature of these conflicts was the extreme brutality with which each group sought to achieve its aims. It is estimated that more than 1,750,000 people—that is, more than one-tenth of the population—perished during this four-year period. It is difficult to determine whether more Yugoslavs died at the hands of the Germans or at the hands of their fellow Yugoslavians. The "ethnic cleansing" that we have witnessed is nothing new. It is part of the tragic legacy passed on by the fathers of the current combatants.

Opposition to German occupation was more easily defined during the period from 1941 to 1944. The two principal groups were the Chetniks, led by Colonel Draza Milhajlović, who were committed to the restoration of the Yugoslav monarchy; and the Partisans, led by Josip Broz, who was known during and after the war by his nom de guerre, Tito. He had become a Marxist while a prisoner in Russia during World War I and was committed to creating a unified Yugoslavia in which nationalist claims were subordinated to Marxist ideology.

Although the two groups, the Chetniks and the Partisans, initially cooperated with each other against the Germans, their ultimate political objectives were irreconcilable. While both received aid from the Allies, the Chetniks were eventually co-opted by the Germans for two reasons: first, because they wished to avoid extreme German reprisals against civilians, and second, because the Chetniks hated the Communists led by Tito more than they hated the Germans. By the end of 1943, Allied aid to the Chetniks ceased, and the Partisans became the sole recipients of Allied military support. This decision was not made in ignorance of what type of postwar government might emerge in Yugoslavia under Tito; rather, it was driven by the fact that Tito's forces were more organized and committed to actively contesting German control of the region, thereby tying down hundreds of thousands of German troops that would have otherwise been available to oppose the Allies on other fronts.

Several factors contributed to the Partisans' success as guerrillas. Unable to directly confront German military forces, they made the most of the terrain, operating as small units, particularly at night. They specialized in sniping, ambushing, laying mines, and demolishing bridges and roads needed by the Germans to support their occupation. The Partisans maintained strict discipline; cowardice and treason were punished by swift execution. Political indoctrination was stressed at the smallest unit level. The Partisans were also adept at the use of terror against local collaborators and captured German prisoners. This often invited harsh German reprisals against local civilians, which only increased their support of the Partisans. The Partisans and Tito emerged from the war victorious over both their political rivals and the Germans. They proceeded to create a unified Marxist Yugoslavia.

Tito was successful for three reasons. First, he used repression and terror to suppress his opponents. Second, he had a powerful personality and great political skill. Finally, he received extensive financial and military aid from the West after his break with Stalin in 1948. Tito led Yugoslavia until his death in 1980. In the constitution of 1974—the last under which the republic would operate—Tito established a federation of the six republics and the autonomous provinces of Vojvodina and Kosovo. He also provided for his succession by creating a collective presidency, with the office of the president rotated annually among each of the federation's members.

With Tito's death in May 1980, the collective presidency took over leadership of the republic. The 1980s were marked by economic stagnation and the decline of the Communist Party's legitimacy within Yugoslavia. Each of the republics, especially Serbia, experienced a marked resurgence of nationalist sentiment. The rise of Slobodan Milosevic to power greatly accelerated the forces of disintegration. Having risen through the ranks of the Communist Party as a loyal party man who actively purged both liberals and Serbian nationalists under Tito, he embraced Serbian nationalism in the late 1980s as a means of maintaining power. He was aided by the considerable political ineptitude demonstrated by Croatian president Franjo Tudjman, who actively sought to rehabilitate the political status of some Ustache leaders and purge ethnic Serbs from jobs in the Croatian government.

The call for the establishment of a greater Serbia, one in which all Serbians would live, was viewed as particularly threatening by the other republics because such a union could be achieved only at their territorial expense.

The first free multiparty elections in Slovenia and Croatia in 1990 signaled the end of Yugoslavia. Slovenia and Croatia announced their independence on June 25, 1991, and war began with the Serbian-dominated federal army attack on Slovenia on June 27.

BOSNIA-HERZEGOVINA

GEOGRAPHY

TOTAL AREA: 51,233 sq km

U.S. COMPARISON: Slightly larger than Tennessee

BORDERING STATES: Croatia, Macedonia, and Serbia-Montenegro (Yugoslavia)

GEOSTRATEGIC SIGNIFICANCE: Controls large percentage of land routes from Western Europe to Aegean Sea and Turkish straits

NOTE: Under the Dayton Peace Accords the territorial integrity of Bosnia is agreed to by the signatories.

BOSNIA-HERZEGOVINA

The country will become a confederation with a central government with federated states consisting of the Bosnian government and the Bosnian Serb Republic. Accurate population figures are difficult to estimate because of four years of intense fighting and population expulsions.

POPULATION

TOTAL POPULATION: 3,201,823 (July 1995 est.); 0.65% growth rate (July 1995 est.)

ETHNIC COMPOSITION: Muslim, 38%; Serbian, 40%; Croat, 22%

RELIGION: Slavic Muslim, 40%; Orthodox Christian, 31%; Roman Catholic, 15%; Protestant, 4%; other, 10%

LITERACY: 85% (1981 est.)

GOVERNMENT

TYPE: Emerging democracy with dual autonomous regions

CAPITAL: Sarajevo

PRESIDENT: Alija Izetbegovic

PRIME MINISTER: Haris Silajdzic

BOSNIA-HERZEGOVINA

SUFFRAGE: From age 16, if employed; universal at age 18

ECONOMY

CURRENCY: Croatian kuna in Croatian-populated area; Yugoslavian dinar elsewhere

INDUSTRIES (PREWAR): Steel production, mining, manufacturing, textiles, tobacco, and wood finishing

AGRICULTURE: Regularly produces less than 50% of internal needs

NOTE: Due to four years of war and almost complete devastation of the local economy, most significant economic figures are unavailable. The war has effectively destroyed the economy; many cities are completely leveled.

MILITARY

BRANCHES: Army

MANPOWER AVAILABILITY: Males 15–49 years of age, 815,055; 657,454 fit for military service; 38,201 males reach military age (19) annually (1993 est.). Casualties of the current conflict are difficult to estimate. A figure of 200,000 to 250,000 may be reasonable. Up to 60% of the population may be refugees.

CURRENT DISPUTES

Long-term viability of central government in question. Serbia and Croatia will continue to be interested in eventual annexation of territory.

CROATIA

GEOGRAPHY

TOTAL AREA: 56,538 sq km

U.S. COMPARISON: Slightly smaller than West Virginia

BORDERING STATES: Bosnia-Herzegovina, Hungary, Serbia-Montenegro (Yugoslavia), and Slovenia

GEOSTRATEGIC SIGNIFICANCE: Controls a large percentage of land routes from Western Europe to the Aegean Sea and the Turkish straits

NOTE: As of this writing, the eastern portion remains

CROATIA

under Croatian Serb control, but it is to be restored to Croatian control in 1996.

POPULATION

TOTAL POPULATION: 4,665,821 (July 1995 est.)

ETHNIC COMPOSITION (PREWAR): Croat, 78%; Serb, 12%; Slavic Muslim, 0.9%; Hungarian, 0.5%; Slovenian, 0.5%; other, 8.1%

RELIGION: Roman Catholic, 76.5%; Orthodox Christian, 11.1%; Slavic Muslim, 1.2%; Protestant, 1.4%; other and unknown, 9.8%

NOTE: Significant changes in ethnic and religious makeup have occurred since the Croatian recapture of the Krajina region.

LITERACY: 97% (1991 census)

GOVERNMENT

TYPE: Parliamentary democracy

CAPITAL: Zagreb

PRESIDENT: Franjo Tudjman

PRIME MINISTER: Nikica Valentic

CROATIA

SUFFRAGE: From age 16, if employed; universal at age 18

ECONOMY

CURRENCY: Croatian kuna

GDP: $12.4 billion; per capita, $2,640; real growth rate, 3.4% (1994 est.)

INFLATION: 3% annually (1994 est.)

UNEMPLOYMENT: 17% (December 1994 est.)

EXPORTS: $3.9 billion (1993)

INDUSTRIES: Chemicals and plastics, machine tools, fabricated metals, electronics, pig iron and rolled steel, shipbuilding and petroleum refining

AGRICULTURE: Grains, livestock, and dairy products; Croatia once produced a food surplus, but the war has devastated many areas of industrial and agricultural production

MILITARY

BRANCHES: Ground forces, naval forces, air and air defense forces

MANPOWER AVAILABILITY: Males 15–49 years of age,

CROATIA

1,183,184; 943,749 fit for military service; 32,831 reach military age (19) annually (1995 est.)

NOTE: Military casualties estimated at 50,000 with more than 1 million refugees.

CURRENT DISPUTES

Border disputes with Serbia, which occupies the far eastern portion of the country. Croatia and ethnic Croatian forces occupy approximately one-third of Bosnia.

MACEDONIA

Macedonia has proclaimed independent statehood but has not been formally recognized as a state by the United States.

GEOGRAPHY

TOTAL AREA: 25,333 sq km

U.S. COMPARISON: Slightly larger than Vermont

BORDERING STATES: Albania, Bulgaria, Greece, and Serbia-Montenegro (Yugoslavia)

GEOSTRATEGIC SIGNIFICANCE: Controls major transportation corridor from Western and Central Europe to Aegean Sea

MACEDONIA

POPULATION

TOTAL POPULATION: 2,159,503 (July 1995 est.)

ETHNIC COMPOSITION: Macedonian, 65%; Albanian, 22%; Turkish, 4%; Serb, 2%; other, 4%

RELIGION: Eastern Orthodox, 67%; Muslim, 30%; other, 3%

LITERACY: 89.1% (1992 est.)

GOVERNMENT

TYPE: Emerging democracy

CAPITAL: Skopje

PRESIDENT: Kiro Gligorov (injured in assassination attempt, 1995)

PRIME MINISTER: Branko Crvenkovski

SUFFRAGE: Universal at age 18

ECONOMY

CURRENCY: Denar

GDP: $1.9 billion; per capita, $900; real growth rate, −15% (1994 est.)

INFLATION: 54% annually (1994 est.)

MACEDONIA

UNEMPLOYMENT: 30% (1993 est.)

EXPORTS: $1.06 billion (1993 est.)

INDUSTRIES: Basic fuels, mining, light industry, wood products, and tobacco

AGRICULTURE: Grains, vegetables, and citrus fruits; relatively self-sufficient in food production; one of seven legal producers of opium poppies for pharmaceutical use

NOTE: Macedonia is the poorest of the former Yugoslav republics; inflation and the continuing conflict have made it difficult to form economic ties with its neighbors and to generate foreign investment.

MILITARY

BRANCHES: Army and police

MANPOWER AVAILABILITY: Males 15–49 years of age, 585,403; 474,467 fit for military service; 19,693 reach military age (19) annually (1995 est.)

CURRENT DISPUTES

Although Macedonia recently resolved its dispute with Greece over its name and flag, the possibility for future disputes between the countries exists. Al-

MACEDONIA

though Bulgaria has renounced any territorial claims, the presence of the ethnic Bulgarian population and Bulgaria's previous attempts to conquer Macedonian territory could prompt Bulgarian involvement if disputes with Serbia and Albania develop. The presence of ethnic Serbian and Albanian populations has given rise to concerns that Serbia or Albania may seek territorial gains. In conjunction with the United Nations, the United States has provided 300 troops to monitor Macedonia's borders with both Serbia and Albania.

SERBIA AND MONTENEGRO (YUGOSLAVIA)*

Serbia and Montenegro have asserted the formation of a joint independent state, but this entity has not been formally recognized as a state by the United States.

GEOGRAPHY

TOTAL AREA: 102,350 sq km

U.S. COMPARISON: Slightly larger than Kentucky

BORDERING STATES: Albania, Bosnia-Herzegovina,

---

* Serbia and Montenegro were separate republics within the former Yugoslavia. Since the breakup of Yugoslavia, the two states have formed a joint independent state, the Federal Republic of Yugoslavia, claiming to be the successor to the former Yugoslavia. Unless otherwise indicated, references to Yugoslavia after 1992 indicate the union of these two republics.

SERBIA AND MONTENEGRO (YUGOSLAVIA)

Bulgaria, Croatia, Hungary, Macedonia, and Romania

GEOSTRATEGIC SIGNIFICANCE: Controls one major land route from Western Europe to Turkey and Near East; strategic location along Adriatic coast

POPULATION

TOTAL POPULATION: 11,1011,833 (Montenegro, 708,248; Serbia, 10,393,585 [July 1995 est.])

ETHNIC COMPOSITION: Serbian, 63%; Albanian, 14%; Montenegrin, 6%; Hungarian, 4%; other, 13%

RELIGION: Orthodox Christian, 65%; Muslim, 19%; Roman Catholic, 4%; Protestant, 1%, other, 11%

LITERACY: 89% (1991 est.)

GOVERNMENT

TYPE: Republic

CAPITAL: Belgrade

PRESIDENT: Slobodan Milosevic (Serbia), Momir Bulatovic (Montenegro), Zoran Lilic (Yugoslavia)

SERBIA AND MONTENEGRO (YUGOSLAVIA)

PRIME MINISTER: Radoje Kontic (Yugoslavia)

SUFFRAGE: From age 16, if employed; universal at age 18

ECONOMY

CURRENCY: Yugoslavian new dinar

GDP: $10 billion; per capita, $1,000 (1994 est.)

INFLATION: 20% annually (1994 est.)

UNEMPLOYMENT: 40+% (1994 est.)

EXPORTS: $4.4 billion (1990); no exports due to sanctions imposed, 1992–1995

INDUSTRIES: Machine building (trucks, aircraft, armored personnel carriers, and weapons), mining, chemicals and pharmaceuticals

AGRICULTURE: Vojvodina Province once produced 80% of the total cereal production of the former Yugoslavia; today production includes livestock, dairy products, citrus, and olives

NOTE: U.N.–imposed economic embargoes and the cost of the war have caused considerable economic damage. Holdovers from the former Communist

SERBIA AND MONTENEGRO (YUGOSLAVIA)

Party have discouraged efforts to move to a market economy.

MILITARY

BRANCHES: Army, navy, and air force

MANPOWER AVAILABILITY: Males 15–49 years of age, 2,846,378; 2,289,505 fit for military service (1995 est.); 83,783 reach military age (19) annually (1993 est.)

NOTE: Serbia and Montenegro took control of much of the heavy weaponry that belonged to the former Yugoslavia.

CURRENT DISPUTES

Yugoslav forces were directly involved in the wars in both Croatia and Bosnia. During the war Yugoslav soldiers also provided extensive support to ethnic Serb forces in both countries. Serbian forces are also used to suppress the significant ethnic Albanian population of the province of Kosovo. Elements of the Serbian leadership have also threatened to intervene on behalf of the ethnic Serbs in Macedonia.

SLOVENIA

GEOGRAPHY

TOTAL AREA: 20,296 sq km

U.S. COMPARISON: Slightly larger than New Jersey

BORDERING STATES: Austria, Croatia, Italy, and Hungary

GEOSTRATEGIC SIGNIFICANCE: Controls major land and rail links into Croatia

SLOVENIA

POPULATION

TOTAL POPULATION: 2,051,522 (July 1995 est.); 0.23% growth rate (1995 est.)

ETHNIC COMPOSITION: Slovene, 91%; Croat, 3%; Serb, 2%; Muslim, 1%; other, 3%

RELIGION: Roman Catholic, 96%; Slavic Muslim, 1%; other, 3%

LITERACY: 99.2%

GOVERNMENT

TYPE: Emerging democracy

CAPITAL: Ljubljana

PRESIDENT: Milan Kucan

PRIME MINISTER: Janez Drnovsek

SUFFRAGE: From age 16, if employed; universal at age 18

ECONOMY

CURRENCY: Tolar

GDP: $16 billion; per capita, $8,110; real growth rate, 4% (1994 est.)

INFLATION: 20% annually (1994 est.)

SLOVENIA

UNEMPLOYMENT: 9% (1994 est.)

EXPORTS: $6.5 billion (1994 est.)

INDUSTRIES: Ferrous metallurgy and rolling mill products, trucks, electric power equipment, chemicals, and machine tools

AGRICULTURE: Cattle-breeding and dairy farming, some grain production; Slovenia is self-sufficient in basic foods but must import many agricultural products

NOTE: Slovenia is the most prosperous of the former Yugoslav republics, with strong links to Western European economies. Suffered limited damage during a ten-day war with Yugoslav army. Expected to enjoy economic growth.

MILITARY

BRANCHES: Slovene Defense Force

MANPOWER AVAILABILITY: Males 15–49 years of age, 542,815; 434,302 fit for military service; 15,350 reach military age (19) annually (1995 est.)

CURRENT DISPUTES

Gained independence from Yugoslavia in 1991 during a ten-day war

CHAPTER 4

SERBIA: KEY TO WAR AND PEACE

To understand the wars in Bosnia and Croatia, and to recognize the possibility that the war will reignite and spread if the Dayton Peace Accords fail, we must gain some understanding of the Serbs.

As the largest of the former republics in geographic size, population, and military strength, Serbia has both the ability and the historical disposition to attempt to dominate all of the former republics with which it shares borders. The presence within Serbia of large ethnic minorities—principally Albanians in the province of Kosovo and Hungarians in the province of Vojvodina—and their treatment by the Serbs may very well bring Serbia into direct conflict with neighboring states that are not participants in the current wars.

Prior to the NATO bombing campaign in August and September 1995, neither the European nations nor the United States were willing to intervene directly with force in the Bosnian war; therefore, the substantive decisions regarding war, the conditions of peace, and the continued use of genocide as an instrument of national policy were for the most part made in Belgrade. The peace accords themselves would not have been possible if Serbia and its president, Slobodan Milosevic, had not agreed to make concessions for the Bosnian Serbs—a decision motivated not by altruism but by Milosevic's understanding of both internal and international realpolitik. If the last four years are any example of the quality of Serbian decisions and the leaders who make them, the prospects for the peace accords are at best questionable. The likelihood of future conflict in the region on a much larger scale and marked by even greater brutality will remain high in the foreseeable future.

THE KEY TO SERBIA'S FUTURE LIES IN THE PAST

We must look to the past to understand Serbian policy and attempt to forecast its future intentions. Its past reveals Serbia's perception of itself as a martyr and as a nation confident of its ultimate triumph. The Serbs migrated to the area in the seventh century and accepted Christianity in A.D. 879. For most of the next three hundred years, Serbia was governed internally by clans, while externally the Bulgar and Byzantine empires vied for control or loyalty of local clan leaders.

By the twelfth century, a coherent Serbian state had emerged under the leadership of the Nemanja clan, and Serbia came to enjoy a period of independence while it expanded its borders into areas that form parts of modern day Albania, Bosnia, Croatia, Macedonia, and Greece. This period of the Serbian Empire was marked by significant cultural achievement, principally reflected in its churches and monasteries. Politically, however, the country was troubled by internal instability as rival clans continued to fight for control. Internal developments were halted by the rise of the Ottoman Turks, who, as they expanded westward, changed the course of history for Serbia, the Balkans, and Europe for the next five hundred years.

The defining moment in Serbian history occurred on June 28, 1389. Serbian forces under the leadership of Prince Lazar met those of Ottoman Sultan Murad I at Kosovo Polje in what is now the Serbian province of Kosovo. The Serbs were overwhelmed by Ottoman cavalry. As the tide of battle was turning against them, a Serbian knight, Milosh Obilich, deserted to the Turks. When he was brought before the sultan to pay tribute, Obilich drew a hidden dagger and killed the sultan (perhaps the first Balkan incident in which a peace offering was used to provide cover to hostile intentions). Murad was succeeded by his son, Bayezit, who, after killing Obilich, completed the defeat of the Serbs. Later, Bayezit beheaded Lazar and left the dead and wounded Serbian troops to be eaten by scavenging birds. To this day that battlefield is known as the Field of the Blackbirds.

There is a Serbian legend regarding this battle and its significance. On the eve of battle, a messenger from the Mother of God appeared to Lazar and asked him to choose between an earthly empire and the kingdom of heaven. Lazar chose heaven and, after building a church and giving his forces the Eucharist, went forth to accept martyrdom at the hands of the Turks. Defeat became the means of Serbian redemption, and because of their faith, the Serbs believed that one day Serbia would be restored to its past glory and have revenge on its enemies. While all of Serbia was not completely conquered until 1453, for all intents and purposes the Serbian empire died on the Field of the Blackbirds. Serbia and the rest of the Balkans were plunged into a period of occupation from which they did not emerge until the nineteenth century.

Serbia, like many of the other Balkan countries, endured oppression under Ottoman rule. The Serbs were able to preserve their culture by accepting second-class status within the Ottoman Empire rather than converting to Islam. Furthermore, the terrain of the region made total suppression impossible. Some people in the region did convert to Islam, however, under the threat of persecution or as a means to avoid the oppressive taxes paid by non-Muslims within the empire. To this day, Serbs pejoratively refer to the local Muslim population as "Turks," and Serbian hostility toward Bosnian Muslims and ethnic Albanians within Serbia stems in large part from what they believe was betrayal of the true faith by their ancestors over six hundred years ago.

Five hundred years passed before Ottoman power in the region waned; Serbia reestablished its autonomy in 1830, and then gained full independence in 1878. During the almost ninety years between autonomy and the start of World War I, Serbia lived under a constitutional monarchy plagued by authoritarianism and internal instability; its independence was guaranteed only by Russian influence.

World War I began when a Serbian nationalist assassinated Austrian Archduke Ferdinand in Sarajevo on June 28, 1914, leading Serbia into a disaster in which more than 20 percent of its population was killed. World War I also marked the emergence of the Serbians' notion of disproportionate sacrifice and betrayal at the hands of those they had helped.

Many Serbs believe their problems are caused by the misdeeds of others, thus justifying Serbia's actions.* From a Serbian nationalist perspective, the Croats and

---

* The Memorandum of the Members of the Serbian Academy of Science and Art, published in September 1986 and suppressed by the then Communist government of Yugoslavia, is perhaps the best statement of this point of view. This document became the intellectual basis for the Serbian nationalist position when the Milosevic government assumed the mantle of leadership after the collapse of the Communist Party.

Slovenes were ungrateful to the Serbs for freeing them from the Austrians, they refused to accept Serbian dominance of the Yugoslav kingdom, and they collaborated with the Germans. Similarly, the Communists under Tito were ungrateful to Serbia for bearing the brunt of war during the German occupation in World War II. Consequently, the Communists suppressed Serbian nationalism and granted autonomy to the Serbian provinces of Kosovo and Vojvodina. When communism collapsed, the other republics sought to break free of Serbian influence, demonstrating their lack of gratitude for Serbian sacrifices to communism during the period of Communist influence and Serbian efforts to rebuild the country after the war. The international sanctions imposed during the current conflict are seen as an attempt by the world to deny Serbia its rightful claims and as a refusal to restore Greater Serbia to its former glory.

The motto under which the Serbs have fought during this conflict, "Only unity can save the Serbs," illustrates the Serbs' perception of themselves as victims. Unfortunately, it leaves no room for self-examination or for consideration of the claims and concerns of others. Many Serbs believe that their country's internal problems, both economic and political, are the result not of any Serb failing but of the continuing misdeeds of others, whether real or imagined. What was needed for Serbian nationalism in the late 1980s was a leader who understood this Serbian outlook and who was prepared to act. Slobodan Milosevic was this man. Milosevic and other militant Serbian nationalists issued pronouncements about the new order that made the other republics doubtful of any independent future within a new confederation of Yugoslavia. While the republics were preparing to declare their independence in 1990–1991, Milosevic was preparing to make them stay. He supported the war in Croatia and Bosnia because he saw it as an opportunity to maintain and expand his power. While the future of Bosnia will depend upon many factors—the return of a measure of ethnic tolerance, the commitment of the Bosnian and Croat forces to maintain the Bosnian Federation, the world's commitment to rebuild the country, and the Bosnian government's ability to acquire the means to defend itself—Milosevic and Serbia's role in the future of the region will remain crucial.

THE POLITICAL FUTURE OF SERBIA

There appear to be two likely scenarios for the future of Serbian politics. Under the first (the Short Fuse), the Dayton Peace Accords are viewed as a defeat for a Greater Serbia and a betrayal of this dream by Slobodan Milosevic. Widespread organized opposition threatens his control and causes him to overreact. Under the second, Milosevic is successful in portraying the accords as merely a time to regroup while waiting for an opportunity to resume the struggle (the Long Fuse). In both of these scenarios, future activity in the Serbian province of Kosovo and greater internal suppression are likely; the difference will be the matter of degree.

SCENARIO I: THE SHORT FUSE

In the Short Fuse scenario, the people of Serbia, particularly its most vocal nationalists, over the next year or so, come to view the peace accords as a Serbian defeat. Several of the leaders of most nationalist opposition parties in Serbia have already accused Milosevic of treason. Tens of thousands of Croatian and Bosnian Serbs have fled losses on the battlefield and moved to Serbia. They resent Milosevic's failure to aid them when they were under attack and the concessions he made in the Dayton Peace Accords. When the first waves of refugees began to arrive in 1995, Milosevic's government was careful to ensure that they were dispersed and resettled in outlying areas like the Serb province of Kosovo, away from Belgrade, where they could not be organized by opposition forces. If the number of refugees increases due to the Dayton Accords, this resettlement will become more difficult and extreme nationalist opposition parties will grow in strength. This in turn will cause increasing pressure on Milosevic. If opposition reaches a point where he fears he may lose his hold on power, he will be faced with four options: (1) to renew the conflict with Bosnia, (2) to forcibly resettle more of the refugees in Kosovo, (3) to greatly increase the suppression of internal opposition—or (4) a combination of two or more of these factors. The presence of I-FOR forces and a rearming of the Bosnian government make this first option a high-risk strategy. Serbs have just gone through four years of war in Bosnia, their forces suffering significant losses during the last six months of fighting. The losses against either NATO forces or a better-armed Bosnian government would be much higher.

Forcible resettlement may, in the short term, also be viewed as more attractive. As we have seen, Kosovo occupies a place of historical significance in the Serbian national psyche as the heart of the old Serbian Empire and the place in which Prince Lazar and his men paid the price for the restoration of the new Serbian Empire over six hundred years ago. Massive resettlement of this province by Serb refugees is now problematic, however, because ethnic Albanians currently make up 90 percent of the province's population and constitute almost 15 percent of Serbia's total population. Serbian birth rates were exceedingly low even prior to the start of the current war. The losses suffered by Serbs in the current conflict, combined with the doubling of the ethnic Albanian population at the current rate by the year 2000, indicate that if Kosovo is to be retained and resettled, expulsion of the Albanian population must be achieved sooner rather than later. Milosevic or his successors, in order to remain in power and stave off opposition, would have to find a way to maintain the support of a people whose economy has been destroyed by international sanctions and whose dreams of a Greater Serbia have been frustrated. It is possible that Milosevic would return to the theme that helped solidify his hold on power in the first place—namely, the restoration of complete and pure Serbian rule in Kosovo. The "ethnic cleansing" of Kosovo is also a high-risk strategy. The area would have to be cleansed by force, presenting Serbian refugees with the option of leaving one war zone to move into another. It would also result in hundreds of thousands of ethnic Albanian refugees fleeing into Macedonia and Albania, the two states in Europe that can least afford any additional strains on their already fragile existence. Furthermore, despite its small military capabilities, Albania would not likely stand by and watch the slaughter or forced deportation of ethnic Albanians. In all likelihood Turkey and other members of the Islamic community would also become involved. The United States and the European Community would be forced into full-scale action to avoid a complete loss of credibility, given the warnings they have already issued regarding Kosovo and their inaction when the Bosnian Muslims were being "ethnically cleansed." Furthermore, the possibility of independent Islamic action in Europe would have even greater consequences for Western nations—possibly a war between the NATO nations of Greece and Turkey, jeopardizing the Middle East peace process and increasing the likelihood of oil embargoes and terrorism.

The third option involves greater suppression of nationalist forces within Serbia. Although the Milosevic regime has been brutal in dealing with opposition figures and with the independent media during the last four years, rising discontent brought on by an increase in the number of bitter and armed ethnic Serb refugees would demand even stricter measures. The imposition of more repression is also a high-risk strategy. It may in fact lead to an even greater anti-Milosevic backlash and civil war.

Any attempt to combine any of these options will carry the risks associated with any single option. While at present this scenario may seem remote, it should be remembered that authoritarian regimes often miscalculate and risk destroying the nation rather than yield power.

Under this Short-Fuse scenario, the peace accords would collapse even before the NATO forces' withdrawal. This would lead in turn to a renewal of the war in Bosnia. For Europe and the United States, this would mean unavoidable direct involvement in a potentially protracted war at a time when both would rather devote their energies to domestic affairs. This scenario would also mean eventual defeat and devastation of Serbia.

SCENARIO II: THE LONG FUSE

In the second scenario, Milosevic seeks to retain power through a careful balancing of competing interests. He will maintain outward support of the peace accords in order to regain international credibility and needed financial aid. He will support aid to the Bosnian Serb Republic for rebuilding in order to avoid another large-scale Serb refugee crisis and to keep alive the hope of eventual annexation of Bosnian Serb territory into Serbia. To accomplish these tasks he will have to purge, suppress, or buy off hard-line Serb opponents of the Dayton Peace Accords. He must also maintain, but not necessarily increase, the pressure in Kosovo if he hopes to avoid outright insurrection, while encouraging as many ethnic Albanians as possible to believe that hope for a better future lies elsewhere. Finally he must hope for significant domestic changes in Russia, a traditional Serb ally. A more assertive Russia will give Milosevic greater leverage in dealing with both external and internal opponents. Early evidence indicates that this is the scenario Milosevic is now pursuing. Balancing of this complexity will be difficult over time. If he fails in any two of its elements, Scenario I will become more likely. Under Scenario II the prospects of the peace accords improve long enough for the international forces to withdraw and give the Bosnian government a chance to create a better life for all of its citizens. Whether it can restore ethnic tolerance and rebuild the country after the international forces leave remains to be seen. What is clear is that the region will remain a potential flash point for many years to come.

CHAPTER 5

A
CHRONOLOGY
OF THE
CONFLICT

The following chronology summarizes the major events of the wars in Bosnia and Croatia. It also includes significant events that have occurred in the other nation-members of the former Yugoslavia. The chronology begins with the declaration of independence of the republics of Slovenia and Croatia in June 1991 and ends with the deployment of U.S. and other NATO forces in January 1996.

1991

JUNE

- Slovenia and Croatia declare their independence from Yugoslavia. Milan Kucan and Franjo Tudjman, respectively, elected presidents.

- The Yugoslav federal army invades Slovenia to prevent separation.

- Slovene forces resist Yugoslav forces in a ten-day war. European Community negotiates a settlement, and Yugoslav forces withdraw from Slovenia in July.

- Ethnic Serbs in Croatia, with support from Serbian forces, begin war and quickly seize approximately one-third of the country. Systematic "ethnic cleansing" by Serbians is reported.

- Ethnic Albanians in the Serbian province of Kosovo vote for independence from Serbia in a possible first step toward unification with Albania. The Serbian minority in the province, with support of the Serbian army, vows to crush any attempt to break away.

JULY

- War continues between Croatian government and Croatian Serbs supported by Yugoslav forces.

SEPTEMBER

- Macedonia votes for independence from the former republic of Yugoslavia and seeks international recognition.

- Bosnian government begins to consider declaring independence from former republic of Yugoslavia.

- The U.N. Security Council imposes an arms embargo on all of the former republics at the request of the Yugoslav government. Embargo locks in Serbian military superiority over the other former Yugoslav republics.

- The Croatian parliament approves a law granting limited autonomy to ethnic Serbs after the end of the war.

- Ethnic Albanians in Macedonia object to Macedonian constitution and threaten to break away in a possible first step toward unification with Albania.

OCTOBER

- Bosnian Serb deputies in Bosnian parliament form Bosnian Serb Assembly.

DECEMBER

- Greece opposes recognition of Macedonia, fearing future territorial claims on Greek province of Macedonia. Macedonia denies any territorial ambition. In a compromise, the U.N. admits Macedonia as the Former Macedonian Republic of Yugoslavia.

- Germany recognizes the independence of Slovenia and Croatia. Other members of the European Community follow.

- Bosnian Serbs declare Serb Republic of Krajina in Bosnian Serb enclave. Rodovan Karadzic elected president.

1992

JANUARY

- U.N. envoy Cyrus Vance negotiates a cease-fire between Croatian and Serbian forces in Croatia. Both sides agree to the deployment of 14,000 U.N. peacekeepers.

MARCH

- Bosnia declares its independence. Alija Izetbegovic elected president.

- War between Bosnian government and Bosnian Serb and Yugoslav forces begins.

- European Community and United States recognize Bosnian independence.

- Bosnian Serbs declare independence and form Serbian Republic of Bosnia.

APRIL

- Serbia and Montenegro agree to establish the new Federal Republic of Yugoslavia as a successor to the former state. The international community gives little political recognition to the new state.

- Bosnian Serbs aided by the Yugoslav army quickly seize almost two-thirds of Bosnia. Serbian "ethnic cleansing" extends to Bosnia.

- Yugoslav forces withdraw from Macedonia.

MAY

- The U.N. Security Council imposes economic sanctions on Serbia for its actions in Bosnia.

- First large-scale antiwar rally held in Belgrade, Serbia. Protesters demand resignation of Serbian President Slobodan Milosevic.

- Yugoslavia withdraws forces from Bosnia, leaving heavy weapons in the hands of Bosnian Serbs.

- Bosnian President Izetbegovic declares a state of emergency and asks for U.N. intervention. U.N. Security Council declines to intervene.

- Bosnia announces the formation of a national army and gains admission to the United Nations.

- Election held in Serbian province of Kosovo. Ibrahim Rugova elected president. Yugoslav army bars inaugural session of Kosovo Parliament.

JUNE

- Yugoslav parliament elects Dobrica Cosic president. He appoints a Serbian-born American businessman, Milan Panic, prime minister. Panic states that his goals are to end the war in Croatia and Bosnia and reduce tensions within Serbia. These efforts are undermined by Slobodan Milosovic, president of Serbia.

- U.N. dispatches 1,000 peacekeepers to secure Sarajevo airport in Bosnia for delivery of humanitarian aid.

JULY

- U.N. reinforces Sarajevo airport with 500 additional peacekeepers.

- Detention camps discovered in Bosnia.

- Ethnic Croatians, former allies of Bosnian Muslims, announce formation of an independent state within Bosnia, the Croatian Union of Herzeg-Bosnia, led by Mate Boban. The Croatian Union favors eventual unification with Croatia. War breaks out between Bosnian government and Bosnian Croat and Croatian forces.

- Yugoslavia rejects European Community mediation of Kosovo dispute. Serb-American Milan Panic elected prime minister of Yugoslavia.

AUGUST

- U.N. Resolution 770 authorizes member states to take "all measures necessary" to assist in the delivery of relief supplies.

- U.N. demands access to camps in Bosnia; all groups condemned for "systematic brutality."

- An international conference on the former Yugoslavia is convened, chaired by U.N. envoy Cyrus Vance and E.C. envoy Lord David Owen.

- Yugoslav Prime Minister Panic ends state of emergency in Serb province of Kosovo.

- Turkey and other members of the Islamic Conference Organization call for limited international intervention on behalf of the Bosnian Muslim population.

SEPTEMBER

- U.N. Security Council enlarges mandate in Bosnia and authorizes the use of force to protect aid convoys.

OCTOBER

- The U.N. establishes a War Crimes Commission to investigate atrocities, amid continuing reports of mass rape, torture, starvation, and executions by all sides, particularly the Serbian forces.

- NATO forces under U.N. authorization are deployed to Bosnia.

- U.N. Security Council institutes a no-flight zone over Bosnia.

- Bosnian Serb and Croatian Serb republics seek union with Serbia.

- European Community threatens sanctions against Croatia for its role in Bosnian war.

NOVEMBER

- The U.N. authorizes member states to enforce the Serbian embargo on the high seas.

- Croatia asserts its right to protect ethnic Croats in Bosnia and signs a cease-fire with Serbian forces, although it had previously denied that any Croatian forces were present in Bosnia.

- The United States threatens air strike to enforce no-flight zone over Bosnia.

DECEMBER

- Milan Panic runs against Slobodan Milosevic for president of Serbia. Panic loses election in which Milosevic controlled the Serbian media. Right-wing nationalists win almost a third of the seats in the new Serbian Parliament and call for the establishment of a Greater Serbia.

- The United States identifies persons suspected of war crimes, including Serbian President Milosevic, Vojislav Seselj, leader of the Serbian Radical Party, and Serbian Member of Parliament Zaljko Raznjatovic (Commander Arkan), a convicted bank robber who is wanted abroad.

- The United States warns Serbia against expanding the conflict to Kosovo.

- The U.N. deploys 700 peacekeepers to monitor Serbian borders with Albania and Kosovo.

1993

JANUARY

- Croatia violates the cease-fire and attacks ethnic Serb positions inside Croatia. Ethnic Serb forces break into heavy weapons depots to retrieve their weapons. Several U.N. peacekeepers are killed in the cross fire. Yugoslavia threatens to intervene.

- The Vance-Owen peace plan is presented to divide Bosnia into ten autonomous provinces under a decentralized federal government. Bosnian Croat forces accept the plan, but it is rejected by the Bosnian government and Bosnian Serb forces.

FEBRUARY

- The U.N. extends deployment of international troops in Croatia for thirty days. Establishes War Crimes Tribunal to investigate and prosecute crimes committed in former Yugoslav republics since January 1, 1991.

- The United States begins air-dropping relief supplies to starving Muslims after Serbian forces deny safe passage for aid convoys in besieged areas.

MARCH

- Bosnian government and Bosnian Croats agree to modification of the Vance-Owen plan and signal acceptance.

- The U.N. extends deployment of protection forces for ninety days and reaffirms support for Croatia's territorial integrity. Authorizes NATO to enforce no-flight zone over Bosnia.

APRIL

- A new wave of Muslim and Bosnian Croat fighting in central Bosnia causes hundreds of deaths and precipitates renewed "ethnic cleansing" by Croats and Bosnians.

- The U.N. designates the Muslim enclave of Srebrenica a "safe area."

- Serbian President Milosevic, threatened with tighter economic sanctions, agrees to support Vance-Owen peace plan.

- Bosnian Serb Parliament rejects Vance-Owen peace plan in favor of a referendum of Bosnian Serbs on the proposal.

- The United States proposes lift-and-strike option—lift arms embargo against Bosnian government and support its ground forces with airpower. European Community rejects proposal.

MAY

- As expected, Bosnian Serbs reject the Vance-Owen plan.

- Serbian President Milosevic's government condemns the Bosnian Serb rejection of the Vance-Owen plan. He vows to cut off all military assistance. Right-wing forces in Serbia vow to defy Milosevic.

- The U.N. Security Council designates five additional Bosnian cities (Sarajevo, Bihac, Tuzla, Goradze, and Zepa) in Bosnia as safe areas effective July 22. Attacks on safe areas continue.

- The United States, Russia, Spain, France, and Great Britain sign a communiqué opposing lifting the arms embargo against the Bosnian government and opposing outside intervention in the war in Bosnia.

- Croatia warned it faces economic sanctions if it fails to stop ethnic Croat forces from attacking Muslim enclaves. Croatian forces now control almost one-third of Bosnian territory.

JUNE

- General Zivota Panic and Serbian defense ministry officials hold secret meetings with Libyan Defense Ministry.

- Bosnian Croats and Bosnian Serbs increase offensive operations against Bosnian government to increase holdings in the event of partition.

- Reports surface that Bosnian military commanders are considering the use of chlorine gas as a last resort to avert military defeat.

- Thorvald Stoltenberg of Norway replaces Cyrus Vance as U.N. mediator. New peace proposal provides for division of Bosnia into three ethnic entities. Plan accepted by Croatia and Yugoslavia but rejected by Bosnian government.

JULY

- The first contingent of U.S. troops arrives in Macedonia to support U.N. monitoring operations on Macedonian borders with Serbia and Albania. Size of U.S. contingent is projected to reach 300.

- Serbian government indicates it will no longer allow CSCE (Conference on Security and Cooperation in Europe) monitors in Kosovo, Vojvodina, or Sandzak.

- The Serbian defense minister holds secret meetings with Iraqi Defense Ministry regarding evading U.N. sanctions and dealing with possible Western military intervention.

- French U.N. peacekeepers come under Serbian attack.

- Firket Abdic, leader of Muslim forces in Bihac, breaks with Bosnian government and establishes Autonomous Province of Western Bosnia, with support from Bosnian Croats and Bosnian Serbs. Fighting breaks out between Abdic's forces and Bosnian government.

AUGUST

- A third major European plan is proposed based on the Serb-Croatian model. It calls for partition of Bosnia along ethnic lines.

- The United States begins air-dropping food and medicine to besieged Muslims facing starvation in Mostar. Croatian forces refuse passage to aid convoys.

- Bosnia makes its case in the International Court of Justice at the Hague, arguing it will be forced to accept the partition plan or suffer further genocide. Serbian representatives claim they are in fact the victims of Bosnian Muslim genocide.

- Reported Serbian arms shipment to Somali warlord Mohammed Adid intercepted aboard a Greek vessel.

SEPTEMBER

- Bosnian parliament rejects Owen-Stoltenberg peace proposal unless Serbia relinquishes additional territory taken during war.

- Bosnian Serb president Rodovan Karadic rejects Bosnian demands for more territory and states that no further territorial concession will be made and that those previously negotiated will be withdrawn.

- U.N. recommends extending protection forces' mandate for additional six months.

OCTOBER

- Forces of Abdic in Bihac seek to end the war based on partition plan and sign peace accords with Bosnian Croat and Bosnian Serb governments.

- Serbian President Slobodan Milosevic dissolves parliament and calls for new legislative elections in December. Milosevic cites "the paralysis of the decision-making process" in parliament, resulting from its unwillingness to censure Serbian Radical Party leader Vojislav Seselj.

- The United States and Albania announce a new military relationship in which the United States will train Albanian military forces.

- U.N. military command in Bosnia reports a massacre of the Bosnian Muslim population of the village of Stupni Do. U.N. officials believe the massacre was perpetrated by the Croatian nationalist army of Bosnia. U.N. forces were fired upon several times before being allowed to enter the village. Evidence indicates that the massacre was preceded by rape and torture of the residents by Croatian forces.

NOVEMBER

- Representatives of the European Union, meeting in Luxembourg, offer a peace proposal drafted by Germany and France, which threatens to cut off humanitarian aid to the Bosnian government if it fails to agree to terms. Parties cannot agree to territorial divisions.

DECEMBER

- Bosnian Serbs refuse to accept U.N. administration of Sarajevo or to reopen Tuzla airport for humanitarian aid.

- Croatian Serbs hold elections. Milan Martic elected president of Serb Republic of Krajina. Cease-fire reached between Croat government and Croatian Serbs.

1994

JANUARY

- NATO summit convenes to discuss the use of an air strike to lift the siege of Sarajevo. Bosnian Serb forces announce total mobilization.

- Croatia and Yugoslavia announce their intention to normalize relations.

- Croatia signals its intention to intervene in Bosnia on behalf of Bosnian Croats.

FEBRUARY

- Sixty-eight civilians killed in Sarajevo marketplace massacre when Bosnian Serbs launch mortar strike into bread lines.

- The United States and France propose ultimatum to Bosnian Serb forces in response to marketplace attack, threatening air strikes if heavy weapons are not removed from a 20-kilometer exclusion zone surrounding Sarajevo or put under U.N. control. Russia intervenes to obtain Bosnian Serb compliance. City remains blockaded.

- NATO shoots down four Bosnian Serb aircraft for violating the no-flight zone, marking the first offensive action by NATO in its history.

- Bosnian Serbs begin shelling U.N. safe areas.

- The U.N. confirms the presence of 5,000 Croatian soldiers in Bosnia. The U.N. threatens sanctions against Croatia.

- U.N. high commissioner for refugees accuses Bosnian Serbs of "ethnic cleansing" in Banja Luka.

- Bosnian government and Bosnian Croats end hostilities and announce the formation of a federation through talks sponsored by the United States.

APRIL

- Bosnian Serbs renew shelling of U.N. safe area in Goradze. NATO air strikes follow. Bosnian Serbs continue their assault, and Goradze falls to Bosnian Serbs. Russians criticize Bosnian Serbs for capture of Goradze, and Bosnian Serb forces withdraw.

- The United States, France, Germany, Great Britain, and Russia form a "contact" group to propose new peace settlements.

- Political opposition to Croatia's involvement in Bosnia grows, due to perceived anti-Muslim views of President Tudjman and his Defense minister. Opposition party formed in Croatian parliament.

MAY

- Croatian defense minister resigns. He was viewed as an obstacle to new federation deal between Bosnian and Croatian governments. Liberal opposition to President Tudjman grows when new Croatian currency, the kuna, is introduced. The kuna was used by the German Ustache government during World War II.

- U.S. Senate votes to unilaterally lift arms embargo against Bosnian government. Diplomatic tension between the United States and other NATO allies increases.

- France threatens to withdraw its U.N. peacekeepers if the arms embargo is unilaterally lifted and if a unified NATO approach is not achieved. First meeting of assembly of the new Bosnian Confederation is held.

JUNE

- U.S. House of Representatives votes to unilaterally lift the arms embargo. Crisis develops between Congress and the president over U.S. policy in Bosnia. U.S. Senate reconsiders previous resolution and withdraws support for a unilateral lifting of the arms embargo.

- First reports of Bosnia receiving arms despite the embargo; Iran identified as possible source.

- A one-month cease-fire is arranged by Bosnian U.N. mediator Yashui Akashi.

- Fighting resumes between Bosnian government and Bosnian Muslims led by Firket Abdic in Bihac.

JULY

- Contact Group proposes new peace plan based on a territory division of 51% Bosnian Confederation, 49% Bosnian Serbs, with U.N. administration of Sarajevo, Srebrenica, Goradze, and Brcko. The Contact Group threatens to lift the arms embargo against Bosnia if the Bosnian Serbs refuse to accept the plan. The Contact Group also threatens to lift sanctions against Serbia if the Bosnian government rejects the plan. The proposal is accepted by Croatia and Bosnia, but it is rejected by Bosnian Serbs. The U.N. fails to lift arms embargo against the Bosnian government despite the Bosnian Serb rejection of the plan.

AUGUST

- Serbian President Slobodan Milosevic criticizes Bosnian Serb rejection of the peace proposal. Says Yugoslavia will close its borders to Bosnian Serbs for all purposes except the delivery of humanitarian goods.

- NATO renews air strikes on Bosnian Serb targets after Bosnian Serb attack on U.N. personnel.

- Bihac falls to Bosnian government forces.

- An Iranian cargo jet arrives in Zagreb, Croatia, carrying "humanitarian relief supplies" for the Bosnian government. News reports indicate the cargo contains large amounts of arms and ammunition.

- Tension arises between Bosnian government and Bosnian Croats over the implementation of a federation agreement.

SEPTEMBER

- Fighting between Bosnian government and Bosnian Serbs resumes around Sarajevo. U.N. commander in Sarajevo threatens to recommend air strike against Bosnian government and withdrawal of U.N. forces if Bosnian government doesn't end offensive operations.

- Serbia allows international observers on its border with Bosnia to monitor border closing in return for the easing of sanctions against Yugoslavia.

- U.N. renews mandate for peacekeepers for six more months.

OCTOBER

- Bosnian government forces go through U.N. demilitarized area in order to attack the Bosnian Serbs. The attack is repulsed by U.N. forces.

NOVEMBER

- Bosnian government and Bosnian Croat forces launch an assault on Bosnian Serb position. Bosnian Serbs wage a successful counterattack and reclaim Bihac.

- Bosnian Serbs violate the no-flight zone. The U.N. adopts simplified rules and authorizes strikes on aircraft launched from either Bosnian or Croatian territory.

- The United States announces that its ships will no longer be used to enforce an arms embargo.

- Bosnian Serb leader Karadzic refuses to meet with U.N. secretary general in Sarajevo to discuss Bosnian Serb attack on Bihac, a U.N. safe area.

DECEMBER

- Former President Jimmy Carter arranges a four-month cease-fire between parties, but fighting continues in Bihac area between Bosnian government, Bosnian Serb, and rebel Bosnian Muslim forces.

- The U.N. estimates that since the beginning of the war in Bosnia in 1991, more than 200,000 people have been killed and 2.7 million have become homeless.

1995

JANUARY

- U.N. Yugoslavia Mediator Akashi and U.N.-forces commander General Rose arrange an extension of the cease-fire to run until April. Sporadic fighting continues, particularly in the Bihac region.

- Croatian President Tudjman threatens not to renew international forces' mandate in Croatia when it expires in March.

- The Z-4 Group (European Community, Russia, the United States, and the International Conference on the Former Yugoslavia) is formed to negotiate a settlement between Croatia and Croatian Serb forces.

- Serbian helicopters stage a resupply effort to Bosnian Serbs in violation of the no-flight zone.

FEBRUARY

- Bosnian Serb and Croatian Serb leaders meet to discuss military cooperation in the event of renewed Croatian operations.

MARCH

- Ethnic Albanians in Macedonia seek to organize a referendum on autonomy.

- Yugoslav army forces begin reinforcement of Croatian Serb forces in eastern Slavonia.

- Bosnian government forces begin an assault on overextended Bosnian Serb lines.

APRIL

- Trials of ethnic Albanian police officers in Serbian province of Kosovo begin. Over one hundred former offices are accused of "plotting against the state."

- Serbian President Slobodan Milosevic begins a crackdown on independent news sources. Most Western news agencies are expelled from the country.

MAY

- Croatian government forces recapture portions of western Slavonia from Croatian Serb forces. Croatian Serbs launch a missile attack on the Croatian capital.

- Bosnian Serb forces renew their attacks on Sarajevo. The U.N. threatens air strikes if Bosnian Serbs do not halt use of heavy weapons. Bosnian Serbs refuse; NATO air strikes follow.

- Bosnian Serb forces launch attack on five of the six U.N. safe areas. They take U.N. peacekeepers hostage, chaining several to potential targets such as ammunition dumps.

- The Serbian government condemns hostage-taking.

- U.N. ceases air strikes.

JUNE

- Russia and Serbia arrange for the release of U.N. peacekeepers.

- U.S. Air Force pilot Scott O'Grady is shot down over Bosnia and rescued six days later by U.S. Marines.

JULY

- Bosnian Serbs capture Sbrencia and Zepa. Bosnian Serb Commander General Mladic personally implicated by survivors in mass execution of Muslim men and boys.

AUGUST

- Croatian army forces recapture all remaining territory of western Slavonia from Croatian Serb forces. Rebel Serb forces are defeated in less than three days. President Tudjman invites Croatian Serbs to remain. There are numerous reports of Croatian forces engaged in looting, arson, and murder. Thousands of Croatian Serbs flee into Bosnia and Serbia.

- Bosnian Serb leader Karadzic calls Serbian President Milosevic a traitor for failing to assist Croatian Serbs.

- Bosnian Serbs shell the Sarajevo marketplace. In response, NATO begins Operation Deliberate Force, bombing numerous Bosnian Serb targets. Bosnian and Croatian forces launch attack on Bosnian Serb position.

- Serbian President Milosevic condemns NATO attacks but makes no move to provide military assistance to Bosnian Serb forces.

- Bosnian Serbs authorize Serbian president to negotiate peace agreement on their behalf.

SEPTEMBER

- Operation Deliberate Force continues, with Tomahawk missile strikes on Bosnian Serb positions. Bosnian Serb forces agree to comply with NATO conditions for a cease-fire.

- Croatia, Bosnia, and Serbia reach agreement for future confederation of Bosnia; they also agree to U.S.–sponsored peace talks.

- Agreements signed in Geneva and New York authorize formal peace talks.

OCTOBER

- A cease-fire agreement is negotiated.

NOVEMBER

- Peace talks begin in Dayton, Ohio. The presidents of Croatia, Bosnia, and Serbia attend. Serbia negotiates in behalf of Bosnian Serbs.

- Croatia and Serbia agree to a two-year transition period for the return of eastern Croatia territory to Croatian control.

- A peace accord between Bosnia, Croatia, and Serbia is initialed. NATO pledges 60,000 troops, including 20,000 from the United States, to implement the accord.

- Bosnian Serbs at first reject but later accept the peace accord provisions. Bosnian Serbs in suburbs of Sarajevo vow to resist reunification of the city.

- U.S. advanced forces begin to arrive in Bosnia.

- The U.N. Security Council extends the mandate for peacekeepers in Croatia for forty-five days, in Bosnia for two months, and in Macedonia for six months.

DECEMBER

- Opposition to the accords continues to be voiced by Bosnian Serbs. Some Bosnian Serbs threaten to leave and burn Sarajevo rather than live under the control of the Bosnian government.

- A large number of U.S. Congress members express reservations over the deployment of U.S. forces.

- Deployment of U.S. and other NATO forces begins.

- The formal signing of the peace accords takes place in Paris on December 14.

- Former Yugoslav President Borislav Jovic publishes a book titled *The Last Days of the Socialist*

Federation of Yugoslavia. The book implicates Serbian President Slobodan Milosevic in provoking and prolonging the war in Bosnia. Jovic and six other party leaders are purged from party membership. Jovic says he fears "liquidation" if he publishes further material.

- NATO aircraft draw fire over Bosnian Serb territory in violation of Dayton Accords.

1996

JANUARY

- Most U.S. and NATO forces are in place to begin implementation of peace accords.

CHAPTER 6

A
SUMMARY
OF THE
DAYTON PEACE
ACCORDS

On November 22, 1995, the presidents of Bosnia, Croatia, and Serbia, on behalf of Serbia and the Bosnian Serb Republic, initialed the Dayton Peace Accords. The formal signing took place in Paris on December 14. The peace accords consist of a General Framework Agreement and eleven supporting annexes with maps. The accords have three major aims: (1) the cessation of hostilities; (2) authorization of the military and civilian implementation program; (3) the establishment of a central Bosnian government while barring the participation in that government of individuals serving sentences or under indictment by the International War Crimes Tribunal.

The major aspects of each portion of the accords are summarized below.

GENERAL FRAMEWORK OF THE AGREEMENT

The parties agree:

- To the need to "bring an end to the tragic conflict in the region"

- To ensure the territorial integrity of Bosnia-Herzegovina

- To endorse the military aspects of the peace accords including the implementation by NATO forces (I-FOR)

- To the demarcation of boundaries of the two republics that will constitute the country of Bosnia

- To endorse the civilian aspects of the implementation of the peace accords

- To cooperate with the International War Crimes Tribunal for the former Republic of Yugoslavia in the investigation and prosecution of war crimes

ANNEX 1A:

THE MILITARY ASPECTS OF THE IMPLEMENTATION OF THE PEACE ACCORDS

The parties agree:

- To the presence of NATO forces to implement the military portions of the accords for a period "of approximately one year"

- To require NATO forces to act under the political control of the North Atlantic Council and through a NATO chain of command

- To establish a cessation of hostilities by all parties in cooperation with NATO forces and to refrain from conducting or threatening to conduct hostile actions against any of the parties of the accords. The parties furthermore assume responsibility for all military, police, and armed civilian forces under their control and ensure that they comply with the agreement

- To maintain civilian law enforcement within their respective areas

- To cooperate with the investigation of war crimes

- To refrain from reprisals or counterattacks in the

event of violation by another party and to advise the I-FOR commander of such violations.

- To redeployment of their forces and the establishment of a zone of separation between them

- To the removal of heavy weapons from designated zones

- To provide information on the disposition of their forces, weapons, minefields, and fortifications within their respective zones

Furthermore, the parties agree:

- That the I-FOR commander has the right to compel with force a compliance to the military aspects of the accords and to use such force as he shall deem necessary

- That the I-FOR commander shall have the right to deploy forces on either side of inter-Bosnia dividing lines and throughout Bosnia itself

- That the I-FOR commander can use his forces to help create conditions for the implementation of the civilian portions of the agreement, including securing conditions for free elections; assisting in humanitarian missions; and safeguarding the return of refugees and displaced persons

- That the I-FOR commander shall have the right

to observe, monitor, and inspect any facilities he believes have military capabilities

- That the I-FOR commander and his forces shall have unimpeded movement throughout Bosnia by land, water, and air

All parties also agree:

- To deactivate all air defense and early warning radars

- To establish in conjunction with the I-FOR commander a joint military commission to address military disputes, and the I-FOR commander's decision on such disputes shall be final

- To exchange prisoners of war no later than thirty days after the signing of this agreement

- To comply with the requests of the International War Crimes Tribunal for the transfer of indicted persons currently held under their control in prison camps

ANNEX 1B:

AGREEMENT ON REGIONAL STABILIZATION (ARMS CONTROL PROVISIONS)

The parties agree:

- To the need to establish a regional arms control program and to engage in negotiation to accomplish this end

- To refrain from the importation of any weapons into the region for a period of ninety days from the signature of this agreement while such negotiations take place

- To refrain from the importation of any heavy weapons for a period of 180 days from the signature of the agreement should the negotiation fail to establish a uniform arms control agreement

ANNEX 2:

AGREEMENT ON THE BOUNDARIES OF THE FEDERATION OF BOSNIA AND THE SERB REPUBLIC WITHIN BOSNIA

The parties agree that the boundaries for the subject republic within Bosnia are set forth in the sign map (see

map page 138). They also agree that the final status of
the city of Brcko and surrounding areas shall be settled
by international arbitration to be completed within a
one-year period.

ANNEX 3:

AGREEMENT FOR THE SCHEDULING OF
ELECTIONS FOR THE CENTRAL GOVERNMENT OF
BOSNIA

The parties agree to the holding of free and fair elections
for offices under the new constitution for the central Bosnian government.

They also agree that the elections will be held no
sooner than six months and no later than nine months
after signature of this agreement, and that they shall be
monitored by international monitors and subject to uniform rules for the conduct of campaigns.

ANNEX 4:

THE CONSTITUTION FOR THE CENTRAL
GOVERNMENT OF BOSNIA

The parties agree that there shall be a written constitution for the central government of Bosnia. The provisions
of the constitution will include:

- The right of all refugees to return to their home
  of origin

- Assurances of individual human rights

- The responsibilities of the central government

- The responsibilities of the two republics that will constitute Bosnia, including "the right to establish special parallel relationships with neighboring states consistent with the sovereignty and territorial integrity of Bosnia"

- The establishment of a two-house parliamentary legislature based on provisions of ethnic representation

- The establishment of a three-member collective presidency based on the principle of ethnic representation

- The establishment of a constitutional court whose members are selected on the basis of ethnic representation and appointed by the president of the European Court for Human Rights

- The creation of a central bank to establish a unified monetary policy

- The provision that no person serving a sentence or under indictment for the commission of war crimes shall be eligible to serve in the Bosnian government

- Procedures for amending the constitution

- The incorporation of significant human rights treaties and accords for the protection of human rights

ANNEX 5:

AGREEMENT ON ARBITRATION

The parties agree to be bound by the arbitration provisions of the "Agreed Basic Principles" agreement signed by the parties in Geneva, Switzerland, on September 8, 1995.

ANNEX 6:

AGREEMENT ON HUMAN RIGHTS

The parties agree to be bound to basic international agreements respecting human rights and to the establishment of a human rights commission to investigate and prosecute violations of human rights and to assist other ongoing investigations by the International War Crimes Tribunal.

ANNEX 7:

AGREEMENT ON REFUGEES AND DISPLACED PERSONS

The parties agree:

- To the right of all persons to return to their home of origin

- To ensure the safety of all those seeking to return

- To the repeal of any legislation that discriminates against persons based on race or religion

- To provide information to assist in the location of missing persons

- To the settlement of dispute claims to real property

ANNEX 8:

AGREEMENT TO PRESERVE NATIONAL MONUMENTS

The parties agree to the establishment of a commission to designate, repair, and preserve national monuments.

ANNEX 9:

AGREEMENT FOR THE ESTABLISHMENT OF BOSNIAN PUBLIC CORPORATIONS

The parties agree to the importance of establishing public corporations to provide essential services such as energy, postal services, communications, and transportation to both of the republics that constitute Bosnia.

ANNEX 10:

AGREEMENT FOR THE IMPLEMENTATION OF THE CIVILIAN ASPECTS OF THE ACCORDS

The parties agree to the appointment of a high representative to supervise the implementation of the civilian aspects of the accords.

It is further agreed that this civilian high representative shall have no control, and no power to interfere with, the I-FOR commander and his implementation of the military aspects of the accords.

ANNEX 11:

AGREEMENT ON THE INTERNATIONAL POLICE TASK FORCE

The parties agree to the establishment of an International Police Task Force to assist the Republic of Bosnia with the implementation of the civilian aspects of the peace accords including the provisions affecting human rights, elections, and the investigations of war crimes.

CHAPTER 7

OVERVIEW
OF
OPERATION
JOINT
ENDEAVOR

NATO will be responsible for implementing the Dayton Peace Accords in an operation known as Joint Endeavor. This will be the largest military operation in the history of the alliance. Approximately 60,000 NATO troops in addition to forces from non-NATO nations will be deployed in Bosnia. The U.S. portions of this contingent will consist of approximately 20,000 troops in Bosnia and will be supported by an additional 12,000 U.S. troops based in neighboring countries. Overall command for the mission will rest with U.S. Army General George Alfred Joulwan, Supreme Allied Commander, Europe, and Commander-in-Chief, United States European Command. He will be assisted by U.S. Navy Admiral Leighton W. Smith, Commander-in-Chief, Allied Forces Southern Europe, and U.S. Army Major General William L. Nash, Commander 1st Armored Division. The charts and maps that follow provide an overview of Operation Joint Endeavor. Unless otherwise indicated, the source of this information is the U.S. Department of Defense.

NATIONS CONTRIBUTING FORCES TO I-FOR

NATO COUNTRY	ANTICIPATED CONTRIBUTION
BELGIUM	1,000
CANADA	1,200 – 1,500
DENMARK	1,000
FRANCE	12,000 – 14,000
GERMANY	4,000 – 5,000
ITALY	2,100
LUXEMBOURG	300
THE NETHERLANDS	2,000
NORWAY	750
PORTUGAL	300 – 900
SPAIN	1,000 – 1,500
TURKEY	1,000
UNITED KINGDOM	14,000

NON-NATO COUNTRY	ANTICIPATED CONTRIBUTION
AUSTRIA	300
BANGLADESH	1,250 (UNPROFOR)
EGYPT	(Possible Participation)
ESTONIA	(Possible Participation)
FINLAND	850
CZECH REPUBLIC	800
HUNGARY	(Support Facilities Only)
UKRAINE	(Possible Participation)
MALAYSIA	(UNPROFOR)
LATVIA	(Possible Participation)
LITHUANIA	(Possible Participation)
NEW ZEALAND	(Small Contingent)
PAKISTAN	1,000
POLAND	800
SLOVAK REPUBLIC	(UNPROFOR)
SWEDEN	1,000
RUSSIAN FEDERATION	1,500 – 2,000

Source: DOD 11/30/95

U.S. FORCES PARTICIPATING IN OPERATION JOINT ENDEAVOR

The bulk of U.S. forces will be from the 1st Armored Division based in Germany. They will be augmented by U.S. Navy and Marine personnel. In addition, the Department of Defense has identified the following units or portions thereof for potential participation in Operation Joint Endeavor:

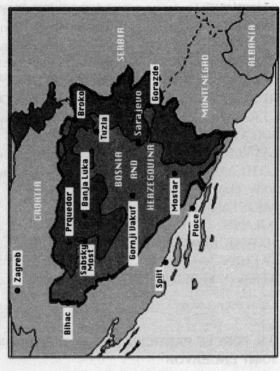

DAYTON-AGREEMENT DIVISION FOR SEPARATION OF HOSTILE FORCES IN BOSNIA

DISPOSITION OF I-FOR FORCES

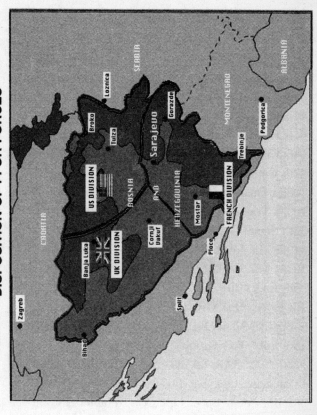

UNIT	LOCATION DEPLOYING FROM

(Active Duty U.S. Army)

UNIT	LOCATION DEPLOYING FROM
4th Batt, 325 Airborne Infantry Reg.	Ft. Bragg, N.C.
362nd Eng. Co.	Ft. Bragg, N.C.
586th Eng. Co.	Ft. Benning, Ga.
54th Quartermaster Co.	Ft. Lee, Va.
41st Explosive Ord. Det.	Ft. Bliss, Tx.
61st Explosive Ord. Det.	Ft. Sill, Ok.
546th Explosive Ord. Det.	Ft. Sam Houston, Tx.
84th Combat Stress Det.	Ft. Carson, Co.
102nd Quartermaster Co.	Ft. Campbell, Ky.
403rd Transport Co.	Ft. Bragg, N.C.
55th Signal Co.	Ft. Meade, Md.
319th Mil. Intell. Bn.	Ft. Bragg, N.C.
303rd Mil. Intell. Bn.	Ft. Hood, Tx.
55th Engr. Co.	Ft. Riley, Kan.
4th Psych. Ops. Group	Ft. Bragg, N.C.
96th Civil Affairs Bn.	Ft. Bragg, N.C.
10th Spec. For. Group	Ft. Carson, Co.
528th Spec. Ops. Sp. Bn.	Ft. Bragg, N.C.
112th Spec. Ops. Sig. Bn.	Ft. Bragg, N.C.
3rd Bn. 160th Spec. Ops. Av. Reg.	Hunter AA, Ga.
1st Special Forces Group	Ft. Lewis, Wa.
5th Special Forces Group	Ft. Campbell, Ky.

UNIT	LOCATION DEPLOYING FROM

(Army Reserve / National Guard)

UNIT	LOCATION
20th Special Forces Group	Birmingham, Al.
353rd Psych. Ops. Bn.	Moffet Field, Ca.
7th Psych. Ops. Group	Moffet Field, Ca.
715th Public Aff. Group	Washington, D.C.
209th Public Aff. Group	Rome, Ga.
49th Mil. History Det.	Forrest Park, Il.
17th Psych. Ops. Bn.	Arlington Heights, Il.
308th Civil Aff. Brig.	Homewood, Il.
186th M.P. Company	Camp Dodge, Ia.
102nd Mil. History Det.	Topeka, Kan.
203rd Public Aff. Det.	Wichita, Kan.
29th Public Aff. Det.	Baltimore, Md.
126th Mil. History Det.	Worcester, Mass.
210th M.P. Bn.	Taylor, Mi.
1776th M.P. Company	Taylor, Mi.
415th Civ. Aff. Bn.	Kalamazoo, Mi.
19th Mil. Mang. Cmd.	Ft. Shelling, Mi.
329th Postal Co.	St. Paul, Minn.
114th M.P. Company	Clinton, Miss.
113th M.P. Company	Brandon, Miss.
1107th Aviation Rpr. Dpt.	Springfield, Mo.
10th Psych. Ops. Bn.	St. Louis, Mo.
1137th M.P. Company	Kennett, Mo.
114th Public Aff. Det.	Manchester, N.H.

UNIT	LOCATION DEPLOYING FROM
361st Press Camp	Ft. Totten, N.Y.
353rd Civ. Aff. Cmd.	Bronx, N.Y.
130th Mil. History Det.	Raleigh, N.C.
326th Mil. History Det.	Columbus, Oh.
23rd AG Postal Co.	Pittsburgh, Pa.
304th Civ. Aff. Brgd.	Philadelphia, Pa.
113th Public Aff. Det.	San Juan, P.R.
90th Mil. History Det.	San Antonio, Tx.
755th AG Postal Co.	Texarkana, Tx.
358th Public Aff. Det.	Ft. Douglas, Ut.
432 Civ. Aff. Bn.	Green Bay, Wis.
152nd M.P. Det.	Moundsville, W.V.
443rd Civ. Aff. Bn.	Warwick, R.I.
19th Spec. For. Group	Salt Lake City, Ut.
305th Rear Ar. Op. Cmd.	Bad Kreuznach, Germany
309th Rear Ar. Op. Cmd.	Friedberg, Germany
Mobilization Sup. Ctr.	Heidelberg, Germany
221st Public Aff. Det.	Heidelberg, Germany
Military Intell. Group	Heidelberg, Germany
310th Theater Army Ar. Group	Kaiserslautern, Germany

UNIT	LOCATION DEPLOYING FROM
330th Tac. Ops. Ctr.	Kaiserslautern, Germany
454th Reg. Replacement Det.	Rhein Main, Germany
317th Rear Ar. Op. Ctr.	Wiesbaden, Germany
663rd Movement Ctl. Team	Vincenzia, Italy
793rd Movement Ctl. Team	Vincenzia, Italy

(U.S. Air Force)

9th Recon. Wing	Beale AFB, Ca.
823rd Civil Eng. Sqd.	Hurburt Field, Fl.
314th Op. Group	Little Rock AFB, Ark.
23rd Aero. Med. Evac. Sqd.	Pope AFB, N.C.
55th Wing	Offut AFB, Neb.

Source: DOD 12/07/95

CHAPTER 8

LEARNING
THE
LESSONS
OF THE
PAST

B efore a nation considers employing its military
forces it must ask itself several questions. First,
what political objectives does the use of forces
seek to achieve? Second, does the nation have the military capability to achieve these objectives based on a
comparison with its own strengths and weaknesses to
those of its potential opponent? Third, do the costs of
engaging in this military operation (the number of cau-
salities, financial expense, and international political impact) outweigh the costs of not acting?

In answering these questions, the policymakers and
their military commanders should evaluate the current
problem in light of historical experience. Although no

two situations are exactly alike, history can teach us important lessons in dealing with current situations and in determining which policies are likely to succeed and which are not. As we have seen, Balkan history offers ample opportunities for assessing the success or failure of political, diplomatic, and military policies.

In selecting historical parallels to the current situation in Bosnia, it is best to choose the ones that most closely resemble the existing situation in terms of the political and military forces at work. In reviewing today's situation and attempting to discern how the crisis developed and what prompted the U.S. decision to intervene, the most relevant parallel would be the aggressive policies of Nazi Germany that led to World War II. As to what lessons the U.S. and NATO forces should be mindful of as they implement the peace accords, those parallels that seem most relevant would be German military operations in the Balkans during that war. While there are some significant factual differences between the two deployments, overall there are substantial similarities between the circumstances that will confront NATO forces and those faced by Nazi Germany.

THE DEVELOPING CRISIS: THEN AND NOW

In purely geostrategic terms, neither Serbia nor any of the Balkan states are comparable to Nazi Germany in its ability to project itself on either a continental or global basis, but the political and diplomatic similarities in the current crisis are striking.

Europe during the 1930s was seeking to resolve the economic and political problems of the Great Depression and the post–World War I period. The new democracies that emerged in Eastern Europe after World War I were extremely fragile. The United States, after spending blood and treasure during the war, had become disillusioned with the intrigues of European politics and had turned inward to deal with its own economic problems while trying to avoid any further entanglements in European affairs. In Germany, Adolf Hitler, having come to power in a democratic election, albeit with serious questions regarding its fairness, established an authoritarian regime and quickly suppressed internal opposition, often brutally. He articulated a foreign policy that was extremely nationalist and racist.

At the outset, Hitler was careful to avoid direct confrontation with other major European powers, but he skillfully played upon their fears of instability, communism, and another war in Europe. His first forays into expansion had as their pretext the treatment of ethnic Germans in a targeted country. He achieved his initial goals, despite clear violations of international law, diplomatic and economic pressure, and concerns expressed in the League of Nations, the precursor of the United Nations.

The other European states, unwilling to put their own forces at risk and directly challenge Hitler's policies, allowed him a free hand in dealing with the countries he first sought to conquer, although they stated their opposition to his aggression and expressed genuine horror at the plight of those brought under German control. The authoritarian states of Eastern Europe took note of Western indifference to the growing German threat. They aligned themselves with Germany, hoping to avoid becoming Hitler's next victims and seeking to follow their own plans for dealing with "enemies" in conjunction with their own expansionist aims. By 1939 Hitler had rearmed Germany, reoccupied the Rhineland, annexed Austria, achieved international acquiescence in his conquest of Czechoslovakia, and coopted the Soviet Union. Hitler's Fascist ally in Italy, Benito Mussolini, had conquered Ethiopia and was reasserting Italy's power throughout the Adriatic and North Africa. Ultimately, Hitler's initial successes proved to be his downfall. They created overconfidence in Germany's military might and the belief that the Western European nations lacked the political resolve to resist his policies. Thus his miscalculations led to his eventual defeat, but not before plunging the world into World War II, which resulted in the loss of more than 30 million lives.

In more recent times, Europe emerged from the Cold War and, after enjoying an all too brief period of euphoria, began struggling to form a new political union and deal with the severe economic problems brought on in part by the victory in the Cold War. The new democracies that emerged from behind the Iron Curtain are extremely fragile and are struggling with both enormous economic problems and the strong authoritarian and nationalist aspects of their political cultures. The United States, after expending enormous human and monetary resources throughout the Cold War, once again began to turn inward to deal with its own problems. It seemed weary of any future involvement in the problems of Europe or the world in general. Operation Desert Storm proved to be a singular example of what the United States and its allies could achieve when vital interests and international law were challenged. Subsequent U.S. involvement in peacekeeping missions in Haiti and Somalia dampened enthusiasm for significant military operations, as did the earlier U.S. peacekeeping experience in Beirut, Lebanon.

In Serbia, Slobodan Milosevic came to power in a democratic election, albeit with significant questions as to its fairness. He quickly suppressed internal opposition, often brutally. He has articulated a foreign policy that is both nationalist and racist. He has skillfully played upon European fears of instability, Muslim extremism, and ground war in the region. From June 1991 until the summer of 1995, using the treatment of ethnic Serbs as a pretext for launching aggressive campaigns, his forces have invaded or directly supported ethnic Serb operations in Slovenia, Croatia, and Bosnia. At the high point of Serbian success Serb and ethnic Serb armies controlled one-third of Croatia and two-thirds of Bosnia. Serbian forces operated in these countries despite clear violations of international law and the diplomatic and economic pressures brought by the United Nations. The major European powers proved unwilling to directly confront Serbian territorial ambitions, although they made strong statements opposing aggression and expressing genuine horror at the plight of those brought under Serbian rule. Furthermore, Serbian aggression and the absence of a consistent and forceful response on the part of Western Europe or the United States supplied a valuable lesson to others in the area and the world illustrating Western European and U.S. resolve. It has also severely strained relations between the United States and its European allies. Serbian success produced overconfidence, which in turn led to miscalculations on the part of Serbian President Slobodan Milosevic (that he could control the Bosnian Serbs and that they would not be a threat to his own power) and on the part of the Bosnian Serb government (that it could act with impunity toward the international community). The taking of U.N. peacekeepers as hostages and the use of them as human shields, the repeated shelling of U.N. safe havens, the acceleration of "ethnic cleansing," and the mass execution of refugees from Srebrenica and Zepa finally provoked a limited NATO response known as Operation Deliberate Force. This response may have been generated by the human carnage caused by Serb actions, the realization that Western credibility was being destroyed, the threat of Muslim nations unilaterally deciding to lift the arms embargo, or growing domestic political pressures within Western European nations and the United States, or by a combination of all these factors. In any event the United States and its NATO allies now determined that the costs of not acting outweighed those of intervening. A coordinated Western military action in conjunction with Croatian and Bosnian successes on the ground produced a cease-fire and the signing of the Dayton Peace Accords.

The United States and NATO have now pledged 60,000 troops to implement this agreement over a period of one year. While there is little enthusiasm for the agreement in the United States, should we not follow through at this time, the hope of maintaining the NATO alliance, the credibility of Western nations to preserve peace and security in Europe, and America's other global security commitments abroad will be seriously undermined.

GERMAN OPERATIONS COMPARED WITH THOSE FACING NATO FORCES

First, there is *no* comparison between the moral and political motives and methods of NATO forces implementing the Dayton Accords and those that underlay Nazi Germany's actions in the Balkans. On a military basis, however, the United States, Western Europe, and ethnic Serbian forces in Bosnia share many of the same advantages and disadvantages that faced the Western Allies and Nazi Germany during different periods of World War II in the Balkan theater of operations.

Germany's decision to invade the Balkans was prompted by the failure of Italy's invasion of Albania and

Greece and the need to secure Germany's southern front before invading the Soviet Union. Planning for the operation was rapid, even by German standards, with the broad outline for the invasion being worked out in twenty-four hours. Despite concern regarding the Balkan terrain and the logistical requirements of supporting the operation, Germany nonetheless enjoyed enormous advantages in terms of equipment and experience in modern combined-arms tactics, airpower, and military leadership.

The German invasion of Yugoslavia began on April 6, 1941, and Yugoslavia accepted unconditional surrender on April 17. The main German combat elements began redeployment on April 21, and Yugoslavia ceased to exist. The Germans captured more than 254,000 prisoners while sustaining only 558 casualties.

Problems arose, however, when the Germans attempted to hold the region and exploit its people and resources for its war machine. At the same time, they hoped to accomplish two nonmilitary objectives that conflicted with their primary military aims. Their first nonmilitary objective was to eliminate the "undesirable" elements of the region's population: Jews, Gypsies, and Serbs. The second was to reconcile the competing territorial claims of their Fascist allies—Italy, Hungary, Bulgaria, and the puppet Croatian state—whose leaders were at times even more brutal than the Germans and did little to contribute to Germany's wartime needs. These conflicting political objectives, along with the difficult terrain and the people's long history of resistance to foreign invaders, created ideal conditions for a guerrilla movement. At the height of this eventually unsuccessful campaign, Germany was forced to commit over 700,000 German troops to the Balkans. One in seven of these troops became a casualty.

After the war, two studies of the German experience in the Balkans were prepared by the U.S. Army's Center for Military History, based on material from German military archives and on monographs and summaries of German commanders. The lessons learned from the German perspective are worthy of consideration. After presenting these lessons, we will discuss the differences and similarities the NATO forces will confront as they implement the accords.

The principal lessons to be learned from Germany's experience in the Balkans include the following:

1. The Germans underestimated their opponents. While the Yugoslav army quickly crumpled in the face of a superior military force, the people of the region had a long history of resisting foreign occupation. They were particularly adept at using the mountainous terrain to make an occupier's attempt to control the region both difficult and costly.

2. Harsh administration of the people by Germany

and its allies only succeeded in creating more guerrillas.

3. The Balkans present an occupier with two tough military problems: counterinsurgency, and military operations in an urban terrain. The former problem predominated during most of the German campaign, and the second presented difficulties as the guerrillas became increasingly successful in capturing populated areas. Furthermore, Germany could dedicate only secondary forces to this area. The combat units that had so quickly accomplished the invasion were withdrawn for use in the invasion of the Soviet Union. Most of their replacements were older men, led by officers whose combat experience was gained in World War I. As the war progressed and the Partisan guerrillas extracted greater casualties, the Germans used as replacements those soldiers who had been wounded on other fronts, had little or no training in mountain warfare, and lacked the stamina to operate in the region. German personnel support for the Balkan theater eroded throughout the war. German attempts to compensate for manpower shortages by relying on the forces of its allies, principally Italy and Bulgaria, were of little avail, as these forces would engage the Partisans only after German units had broken the principal enemy

resistance. These forces later became unavailable when Italy and Bulgaria surrendered, leaving Germany to assume even more responsibilities in the Balkans. German reliance on foreign legions and local collaborators was equally unsuccessful, as these units required extensive German supervision and were of limited combat value and questionable political reliability.

4. There was no effective central control for counterguerrilla operations either among German military and political commanders in the region or among the Germans and their allies.

5. German military units failed to enforce basic security. Logistical problems forced the Germans to rely on local civilians for basic support functions and for much of their food. These civilians were able to observe the disposition of German troops, discover the location of stores and ammunition, and then plan guerrilla operations. As a result almost all German operations were compromised when the outwardly cooperative civilians relayed their information to the guerrilla forces.

6. Germany had no organized propaganda effort designed to explain the advantages of cooperating with their occupation forces.

7. Perhaps the Germans' most devastating mistake

was their failure to offer any hope to the people concerning the eventual withdrawal of occupation forces and the granting of independence. When the local people were confronted with the possibility of either permanent subjugation or a prolonged fight for independence, they chose, as they traditionally have, to fight regardless of the cost.

CHALLENGES FACING NATO FORCES

Today's NATO forces enjoy major advantages over the German forces in terms of entry to Bosnia. First, they have been invited into the country by the parties of the Dayton agreement. Second, the intervention will be NATO's primary effort; unlike German operations during World War II, it will not occur in conjunction with larger military commitments across the continent. Third, the intervention will enjoy at least initially, the support of significant portions of the Bosnian population who seek an end to the war (support will not, however, be universal, and there will be significant opposition from those who view the peace accords as a less than satisfactory solution to their problems, whether for political, ethnic, religious, or criminal reasons). NATO forces face reduced risks of opposition and casualties as they begin the deployment, but the risks will come during the implementation of the accords.

Having discussed the lesson of the German experience in the Balkans during World War II, we can now discuss these points as they relate to the current NATO deployment.

1. The NATO forces do not underrate the existing organized operational capabilities. In terms of numbers, weapons, and military leadership capability, NATO forces could quickly defeat any standard fixed resistance. The terrain advantages an opposing force would enjoy nonetheless remain. German casualties were a product of disease, weather, and small-scale operations— ambushes, mines, sniping, throat cutting, and so forth. NATO forces should not suffer either from medical or logistical reasons. Small-scale actions will, however, be a primary cause of NATO casualties.

2. Unlike German Forces, NATO forces will seek to avoid direct administration of local civil affairs. The peace accords place this responsibility on the local Bosnian entities, the U.N. high representative, and the International Police Task Force. If these parties fail to fulfill their responsibilities, however, the I-FOR commander may be forced to do so simply to protect his forces. NATO forces may also be viewed by local civilians as harsh administrators as a result of I-FOR

responses to attacks on NATO personnel.

3. Although the parties have agreed to invite NATO forces to implement the accords, and although the immediate probabilities of having to conduct counterinsurgency or urban operations are small, the possibility of having to conduct such operations will exist throughout the deployment. Currently no large-scale rotation of NATO forces is planned. This will allow I-FOR troops to get to know their assigned areas. The principal political disagreement among NATO forces will revolve around the training and equipping of Bosnian Muslim forces. While in theory I-FOR is meant to be viewed as a neutral arbiter between the opposing forces, prior NATO bombings of Bosnian Serb positions, and the U.S. commitment to ensure that the Bosnian government can successfully resist future Serb attacks, will surely test this assumption. Military commanders must contend with the essential military need to appear neutral while long-term political and military reality requires that future conflicts can be avoided only if Bosnian government and Bosnian Serb forces are more evenly matched.

4. The question of a central command in control of military actions is resolved by giving the I-FOR commander sole authority to implement

the military provisions of the accords. The accords specifically bar the U.N. high representative from interfering with the I-FOR commander's military decisions.

5. Basic security concerns will initially be small due to the fact that the I-FOR forces have been invited to implement the accords and because deployment will occur during winter, when weather constraints make military action more difficult. By spring of 1996, however, the need to stress basic security procedures will increase. This is true, first, because spring has traditionally marked the renewal of fighting in Bosnia; second, because a potential opponent will have had sufficient time and opportunity to observe I-FOR positions and methods of operation; and, finally, because by springtime the most difficult parts of the peace accords—the return of civilian populations, the investigation of mass graves, the rebuilding efforts, and so on—will begin to be implemented. All of this will bring I-FOR troops into greater contact with the Bosnian population.

6. Because the Germans' plan for the Balkans included conquest and the elimination of elements of the population, there was little in the form of a positive message they could offer to the people under their rule. The Dayton Peace Accords, at the very least, hold out the possibility of an end

to the war and the reconstruction of the country. The success or failure of the I-FOR mission will rest in part in the ability of the United States and Western European nations to convince the parties, through economic, educational, legal, and militaristic means, that life under the peace accords will be better than a renewal of the conflict. The political and moral message that NATO must repeatedly send is one of ethnic tolerance. I-FOR must make a concerted effort to rebut ethnic propaganda while ensuring a balance of military forces that will discourage a renewal of hostilities.

7. Unlike Germany, NATO has pledged to withdraw its forces in approximately one year. This can reduce but not entirely eliminate local fears of a prolonged presence of outside military forces.

CHAPTER 9

THE
FUTURE

Over the coming year as the Dayton Peace Accords are implemented, we shall have a chance to assess the commitment of the people and the leaders of the region, Europe as a whole, and the United States to building a lasting peace in the Balkans. The wars in Bosnia and Croatia were the result of either the deliberate policy decisions or the fateful miscalculations of those involved. The costs of these policies and mistakes have only been partially paid for by the death of hundreds of thousands, the physical and psychological suffering of millions, and economic losses that have yet to be accurately determined. There have also been significant intangible expenses; the rule of international law and basic moral principles have been eroded by these conflicts. Although not all of the parties have been equally guilty and the costs have not been equally shared, everyone involved has paid and will continue to pay.

The United States and its NATO allies, in implementing the accords, are making such a payment. How large this installment may be in lives, time, and treasure remains to be seen. Our ability to implement the peace accords will depend on many factors that are beyond our control. We can influence the chances of success, however, if we remember two of the basic lessons we have already learned at the high costs of the two world wars, lessons that have been ignored many times during this conflict. The first lesson is that territorial aggression in Europe, if unchecked, leads to a larger war and threatens the security of Europe and, eventually, of the United States as well. The second lesson is that the use of genocide as an instrument of national policy cannot be tolerated. To avoid a future war in Bosnia we have to ensure that the Bosnian government has the means to resist should Serbia or the Bosnian Serb Republic seek to renew this conflict. We must also support the work of the International War Crimes Tribunal as it seeks to hold the perpetrators of war crimes—whether Serb, Croat, or Bosnian—accountable for their actions; justice for the victims demands no less, and an effective warning against similar actions in the future will not be possible without it.

The task of the United States and the other members of the implementation force will not be easy, nor will it be without risks. The only guarantee is that the risks will certainly be higher in the future if we fail to act now.

APPENDIX I

REPORTS ON WAR CRIMES

Perhaps the most tragic feature of the wars in Croatia and Bosnia has been the practice of "ethnic cleansing." Not since the Nazis' attempt to exterminate Jews and members of other ethnic groups has Europe witnessed such a callous disregard for international human rights law and fundamental human decency. While the deaths in Bosnia are not comparable in number to those that resulted from the Nazis' "final solution," the perpetrators of "ethnic cleansing" have given every indication that this fact is more a result of timing and lack of opportunity than lack of desire. Current estimates suggest that the total number of persons killed in Bosnia alone exceeds 200,000 and that

APPENDIX I

more than 60 percent of the population has been displaced. These figures do not include the casualties of the war in Croatia.

The task of investigating and prosecuting the individuals responsible for these crimes rests with the International Criminal Tribunal for the Former Yugoslavia. Based in the Hague, the tribunal has thus far issued fifty-two indictments and has begun its first proceeding. One of the major requirements of the Dayton Peace Accords is that all of the parties agree to cooperate with the proceedings of the tribunal. The volume of information on the practice of "ethnic cleansing" makes it difficult to briefly summarize this tragedy. This chapter presents a summary of the final report of the U.N. Commission of Experts, whose task it was to study violations of the Geneva Conventions in the Former Republic of Yugoslavia; excerpts from four of the U.S. government reports to this commission; a summary of the CIA reports on the massacres in U.N. safe areas in 1995; and a list of those individuals currently under indictment for war crimes perpetrated in the Former Republic of Yugoslavia.

SUMMARY OF THE FINAL REPORT OF THE COMMISSION OF EXPERTS

The U.N. Commission of Experts examined human rights violations in the Former Republic of Yugoslavia

APPENDIX I

from November 1992 until April 1994, when its functions were assumed by the International War Crimes Tribunal. The commission's efforts during this period produced an extensive record of human rights abuses. The final eighty-four page report is supported by a multivolume annex of over three thousand pages. The full document provides the following information:

1. A summary of applicable international law.

2. A general study of the military methods employed by the warring parties.

3. Detailed descriptions of the practice of "ethnic cleansing."

4. The use of rape and other forms of sexual assault and torture as a weapon of policy.

5. The operation of detention facilities.

6. Methods employed to investigate mass graves.

The commission concluded that there had been massive violations of international laws and that many of these actions were carried out "so systematically they appear to be the product of policy."

The commission's findings were derived from its own investigations and from reports submitted by member

APPENDIX I

states of the U.N. Security Council. The United States has made many such reports. Excerpts from four of these reports follow.

EXCERPTS FROM THE REPORTS SUBMITTED BY THE U.S. GOVERNMENT TO THE U.N. SECURITY COUNCIL REGARDING VIOLATIONS OF INTERNATIONAL HUMANITARIAN LAW IN THE FORMER YUGOSLAVIA*

The incidents related in this appendix describe in graphic detail the terror that is being inflicted daily upon the people of Bosnia-Herzegovina. While war crimes have been committed by all parties to the conflict, it is nonetheless clear that the vast majority of such incidents have been perpetrated by Serbian forces. These reports also make clear that these acts are "part of a systematic

---

* These excerpts are taken from the reprint of these reports contained in "A Report to the Committee on Foreign Relations—United States Senate" by Senator Joseph R. Biden and titled, *To Stand against Aggression: Milosevic, The Bosnian Republic, and the Conscience of the West*, April 1993. The full reports and the methodology by which these reports were assembled are contained in Addendum D of that document. Representative incidents were selected from the reports dated September 23, 1992; October 22, 1992; November 6, 1993; and March 9, 1993. All those incidents contained in these reports and directed against Serbs have been included. Unless otherwise indicated, the events took place in 1992 and are arranged chronologically, with the most recent events covered in each report being listed first. The sources for the reports are indicated at the end of each entry. (DOS stands for the U.S. Department of State.)

APPENDIX I

campaign toward a single objective—the creation of an ethnically 'pure' state."

WARNING!

The reader is advised that the incidents reported herein contain descriptions of torture, sexual assault, and murder. Those persons who are sensitive regarding the discussion of these topics are warned not to read the remaining portions of this section.

ADDENDUM D: REPORTS BY THE U.S. GOVERNMENT TO THE U.N. CONCERNING VIOLATIONS OF HUMANITARIAN LAW IN YUGOSLAVIA

FIRST REPORT
(SEPTEMBER 23, 1992)

FORMER YUGOSLAVIA:
GRAVE BREACHES OF THE FOURTH GENEVA
CONVENTION

In paragraph 5 of Resolution 771 (1992), the U.N. Security Council called upon all states and international humanitarian organizations to collate substantiated information . . . relating to the violations of humanitarian

APPENDIX I

law, including grave breaches of the Geneva Conventions, being committed in the former Yugoslavia and to make this information available to the council. This report is in response to that request.

WILLFUL KILLING

August 25. At Manjaca prison camp, south of Banja Luka, 25 bodies of emaciated men, believed to be prisoners, were discovered with their throats cut. The camp was operated by the Serbian Army of Bosnia-Herzegovina under General Ratko Mladic (DOS).

July 24. A former inmate at the Serb-run Keraterm camp in Pridedor, in northwestern Bosnia, said more than 100 prisoners died, due to riots after prisoners were denied water for an unspecified period of time; most suffocated in a crowd of prisoners trying to escape through a window. Others were shot while escaping or summarily executed for participating in the riots (DOS).

June 17. A 37-year-old male from Dobj, the village of Pridjel Goraji, described the killing of seven people and the destruction of the mosque by Chetniks. "Some wore white bands; some wore red caps; some wore JNA uniforms. They beat us with rifle butts" (Congress).

APPENDIX I

June. The Citizens Council of Korzarac appealed for international observers about June 6 claiming that a large-scale massacre had occurred in Korzarac and that truckloads of bodies had been taken away to cover up the crimes committed there (DOS).

May 7. A resident of Brcko told of mass killings during the first week of May when Brcko surrendered to Serb forces with little resistance (DOS).

May 2. A 38-year-old inmate at Djakovo refugee camp in Croatia said that she was taken on May 9 to Luka camp near Brcko, where she saw 10 people being killed every day with rifle butts and bottles. "Two prisoners were required to slap each other. The one who didn't slap as hard was killed. One time I saw them cut off the ears of the weak slapper, then cut off his nose and then kill him by cutting his throat" (Congress).

April 10. A Serb who had been married to a Bosnian Muslim told U.S. embassy officers in Budapest on September 9 that several Yugoslav army tanks had come in to Zvornik on April 10. About 30 masked irregulars, who she claimed belonged to a unit under "Arkan," conducted a house-to-house search for Muslim men by checking identity cards. The Serbs then allegedly cut off the heads, hands, and feet of their victims (DOS).

APPENDIX I

TORTURE OF PRISONERS

June–July. A 60-year-old man signed in as prisoner number 519 in the Bosanski Samac camp. "They hit me with a stick and burned me with cigarettes. They would throw water on me to wake me up so they could continue the beatings. I got pneumonia because of the cold water." On the day he was released, he was beaten in the stomach. A certificate from Slavanski Brod Medical Center showed that he was treated July 5–17 for contusions, fractured ribs, and psychotic depression. He had burn marks on his left arm and a large scar on the top of his head (Congress).

March–May. Two American citizens who had enlisted and served in the Croatian army were incarcerated from March to May in three separate POW camps, during which time they were beaten daily with gun stocks. They also witnessed the daily beatings of other prisoners. The prisoners were subjected to electric shock treatment, use of a stun gun, and sexual assault. Scars and bruises were still evident on at least one of the Americans when he was turned over to the U.S. ambassador in Belgrade (DOS).

APPENDIX I

ABUSE OF CIVILIANS IN DETENTION CENTERS

August 30–31. CSCE mission member John Zerolis, a U.S. Foreign Service officer assigned to the U.S. embassy in Zagreb, inspected the Serb-run prison camp of Manjaca in northwest Bosnia. He observed several thousand prisoners, none of whom were wearing any form of uniform. At that time his group was told by the prisoners that they were noncombatants, that they had been summoned from their homes or simply called to the door, and that they were then arrested. Asked about attempted escapes from Manjaca, the camp commander Lieutenant Colonel Popvic said there had never been any, and there "never would be any" (DOS).

August. Serbian civilian inmates, including a pregnant woman and elderly people are subjected to beatings at the former JNA Victor Bubanj barracks in Sarajevo, a camp run by Bosnian Muslims (Belgrade opposition weekly, *Vreme*).

DELIBERATE ATTACKS ON NONCOMBATANTS

August-September. Rexhep Osmani, president of the Naim Frasheri Teachers Association in Kosovo, has been in jail since mid-August facing undefined charges. Forty-one school administrators and teachers were "brutally treated" during the week of September 1 by Serb au-

APPENDIX I

thorities. Serbian police "opened fire" against high school students in early September at the PEC Technical School Shaben Spahija, according to Kosovo education officials (DOS).

September 6. A convoy of U.N. trucks carrying aid supplies to Bosnian civilians was mortared on September 6. Snipers fired all day at U.N. personnel as they distributed food to the people of Sarajevo (Hamburg, DPA).

WANTON DEVASTATION
AND DESTRUCTION OF PROPERTY

March-July. The Croatian city of Slavanski Brod has been hit by over 10,000 artillery rounds, bombs, mortars[,] and ground-to-ground rockets since March. As of July 16, over 70 civilians had been killed, including 18 children, and over 200 wounded. The 3,000 buildings which had been damaged included 15 percent of local residential housing (DOS).

MASS FORCIBLE EXPULSION
AND DEPORTATION OF CIVILIANS

August 2. Albanian leaders described the Serbian intention of changing the ethnic balance of Kosovo. Since 1989, over 100,000 Albanians have been deprived of their jobs. This fall, 64,000 Albanian secondary school children may boycott classes, refusing a required Serbian curriculum (DOS).

June 2. Serb paramilitaries have destroyed neighborhoods with large Muslim populations and killed some people in the towns of Sanski Most and Prijedor, in northwestern Bosnia. An office of emigration was established in Banja Luka to "facilitate" population transfers, since "more and more citizens of all nationalities want to change their place and area of residence" (DOS).

SECOND REPORT
(OCTOBER 22, 1992)

WILLFUL KILLING

August 27. Croatian paramilitary forces attacked a convoy of buses carrying over a hundred Serbian women and children, according to a peasant woman from Goradze who was in the convoy. She said the Croats killed 53 and left about 50 wounded. She escaped by hiding under bodies. Her son, one of two "Serbian Republic" soldiers with the convoy, was badly wounded but survived (DOS).

July 20. A 31-year-old Bosnian Muslim refugee stated that on July 20 all the men living in Biscani were called out of their houses and forced to lie down in the center

APPENDIX I

of town on asphalt. Serb soldiers beat them with iron bars and forced them to sing patriotic Serbian songs. The most prominent women in the village, about 100, were brought together. As the women were told to disperse, they were shot in the back. The bodies of the women lay in the road for 4 days until Serb trucks came to collect them (DOS).

Mid-May. A Muslim refugee, a butcher by trade and probably in his early forties, spent 27 days at Luka camp outside Brcko, during which time he saw a soldier drag a man out of his building and return after a short time with a blood-soaked knife in one hand and the man's head in the other. The refugee discussed with a U.S. Foreign Service officer in Vienna, Austria, the lack of food—a piece of bread about every 3 days. He witnessed one woman in her mid-thirties die of starvation (DOS).

April. Adil Umerovic, a Muslim, shot a young Serb male on a Goradze street for no apparent reason, according to a young Serbian woman who witnessed the killing. She said the Serb was an unarmed civilian who was handcuffed (DOS).

April–July. Imam Mustafa Mojkanovic of Bratunac was tortured before thousands of Muslim women, children, and the elderly at the town's soccer stadium, according to Imam Efardi Espahic of Tuzla. Serb guards ordered the cleric to cross himself. When Mojkanovic refused, they beat him, stuffed his mouth with sawdust and beer[,] and then slit his throat. The Muslim mufti of Zagreb, Sevko Omarbasic, has said that by the end of July the Serbs had executed 37 imams (*New York Newsday*).

TORTURE OF PRISONERS

May–June. A 52-year-old Bosnian Muslim cleric, whom Serbian military police had arrested on May 16 and subsequently released, was picked up again on May 29 or 30 by a convoy of Serb militia; he had been hiding in the woods. He was interned for 75 days, during which time he was beaten regularly until he bled. The cleric witnessed several public beatings and sexual torture in the camp. He said that several men had been forced by the guards to have intercourse with each other and that the guards cut off some prisoners' hands and penises as a punishment and to frighten the other men (DOS).

ABUSE OF CIVILIANS IN DETENTION CENTERS

April 12–28. A 33-year-old Bosnian Muslim refugee, a machine technician by profession, from Sarajevo and her two children were interned in Manjaca camp near Banja Luka for 16 days. During a September 25 interview with a U.S. Foreign Service officer in Zagreb, she described

APPENDIX I

her first interrogation: Two Serbian camp guards, who called each other Todor and Srbo, beat her and burned her right upper thigh twice with a cattle prod. They raped her in front of her children, a 12-year-old daughter and a 9-year-old son. Afterward she bled badly. Her daughter was raped twice (DOS).

WANTON DEVASTATION
AND DESTRUCTION OF PROPERTY

April–July. According to the head of the Islamic community in Zagreb, 200 mosques were destroyed and another 300 damaged between April and late July. The Bosnian Institute in Zurich estimated that, in areas under Serb occupation, 90 percent of the mosques have been destroyed (*New York Newsday*).

MASS FORCIBLE EXPULSION
AND DEPORTATION OF CIVILIANS

June. Serb forces chartered an 18-car train in an attempt to deport the entire population of Kozluk, Bosnia—some 1,800 people—to Hungary, but Hungary refused to admit them. After four days on board, the villagers were brought to the Palic camp. They were told that "this is part of an ethnically pure Serbian region" and that it was "inconvenient to have a Muslim village at a key road junction" (*New York Newsday*).

APPENDIX I

March 18. A Serbian woman in Goradze lost her right arm when "Muslim terrorists" threw a hand grenade in her home in a mixed neighborhood. (DOS).

THIRD REPORT
(NOVEMBER 6, 1992)

WILLFUL KILLING

October 22. A group of approximately 18 ethnic Muslims was kidnapped near the Serbian town of Priboj on October 22 while traveling on a bus route that took them into territory controlled by Bosnian Serbs. Belgrade newspapers reported on October 23 that the kidnapped Muslims had been killed. A Serb official has admitted that Serb paramilitaries operating in Bosnia basically had free run in the Sjeverin area prior to the police and army intervention after the kidnapping (DOS).

September 24–26. An American freelance writer reported that he saw the bodies of mutilated and tortured Serbs from the villages of Rogosija and Nedeljiste at the Saints Paul and Peter Serbian Orthodox Church in Vlasenica after the lids of about 10 of the coffins were removed by soldiers for viewing: "Some bodies were burned to charcoal, others had fingers cut off on the right hand which the Orthodox use to bless themselves, some were circumcised as a final affront (Serbian Orthodox

APPENDIX I

males in Yugoslavia are not circumcised, whereas Muslims are) some had their eyes gouged out, gaping knife wounds everywhere, and heads were battered beyond recognition, arms, legs broken and severed" (Serbian American Media Center, Chicago).

Mid-August. An elderly Serbian farmer was arrested in the village of Idbar, near Konjic, on May 9. He reported that he was taken to a police station in Konjic, where he stayed for 21 days. He was then moved 6 kilometers away to Celebici, where he said that all of the prisoners were Serbs and all of the guards were Muslims. He said that beatings were carried out frequently by guards from outside the area. The prisoners, mostly young men, were beaten with wooden handles of farm tools or with metal rods.

He reported having witnessed 15–16 ethnic Serbs beaten so badly that they died. The witness was able to identify the camp commander and the most vicious of the guards. He was released from Celebici on August 20 with all prisoners over the age of 60 (DOS).

July 24. Three male Bosnian Muslims witnessed and survived a mass slaughter at Keraterm camp on July 24 when guards opened fire with automatic rifles on a room packed with prisoners. About 150 men were killed or wounded in this one incident (DOS).

APPENDIX I

May–June. About 3,000 men, women, and children were killed during May and June at the Luka-Brcko camp, which held approximately 1,000 civilian internees at any one time. Some 95 percent were ethnic Muslims and the remainder were Croatians. Approximately 95 percent were men. Until May the bodies were dumped into the Sava River. Thereafter, they were transported and burned in both the old and the new "kafilerija" factories located in the vicinity of Brcko. . . . The Serbian police appeared to have administrative control of the camp. . . . Approximately 1,000 people were released from the camp when Serbs vouched with their lives (and signed documents to that effect) that the internees would not leave Brcko, discuss politics, or own weapons. These people were all released within a 48-hour period; thereafter, releases were not authorized. . . . Beatings with clubs were common. A Specijalci soldier used a wooden club with metal protruding from it to kill several people. He forced internees to lick the blood from metal studs. Another shot an individual in the back several times after he carried a dead body behind a third hangar in June, some 50–60 men had their genitalia removed . . . . There was also a torture room at the Luka-Brcko camp. Those tortured were either killed immediately after being tortured or were left to bleed and, if they did not die in 2 to 4 days on their own, shot to death. They were left lying in their own blood in the living areas, and

APPENDIX I

other internees were not allowed to help in any way. People were beaten with clubs to the point that the bones in their faces caved in, and they died (DOS).

May 21. A former employee of the Zvornik medical center reported that he was required to remain on duty in the center from April 8 until his dismissal on May 26. He said that the need for more hospital space for wounded Serbian soldiers eventually led to the mass murder of Muslim patients on May 21. At about 1:00 P.M. that day, he watched as 36 remaining Muslim adult patients were forced outside and shot to death on the hospital grounds.

Shortly thereafter, uniformed and non-uniformed Serbian soldiers moved through the pediatric center breaking the necks and bones of the 27 remaining Muslim children, the only children left as patients in the hospital. Two soldiers forced him to watch for about 15 minutes, during which time about 10 or 15 of the children were slaughtered. Some were infants. The oldest were about 5 years old. The witness said that a Serbian surgeon, who also stood by helplessly, later went insane (DOS).

TORTURE OF PRISONERS

May 26–August 6. A 30-year-old Muslim was imprisoned for over 9 weeks at Omarska camp. He had been

APPENDIX I

apprehended by Serbian forces in Prijedor on May 26. The witness reported having seen the following:

- Prisoners were forced to run across broken glass in their bare feet; when they fell, guards would beat them with nightsticks and iron bars.

- As a punishment administered in front of a group of prisoners, a guard cut off the testicles of a prisoner with a knife; one prisoner was forced, under threat of being executed, to bite off the testicles of another prisoner with his teeth.

- The only water that prisoners had to drink was from a river contaminated by discharges from an iron mine; the water was yellow, the prisoner's urine ran red (DOS).

ABUSE OF CIVILIANS IN DETENTION CENTERS

May–Aug. A 41-year-old Croatian female from Kozarc, a 40-year-old Muslim male from Prijedor, and a 39-year-old Muslim male were interned for approximately 3-month periods at Omarska camp. All three subjects claim to have witnessed severe beatings, sexual torture, mutilation, and killing in part because they had spent such long periods in the camp. They are able to identify

APPENDIX I

what they believed to be virtually the entire personnel structure of Omarska camp (DOS).

DELIBERATE ATTACKS ON
NON-COMBATANTS

By October five members of UNPROFOR contingent in Sarajevo had been killed by combatants. In one incident, two French soldiers were killed by fire from Bosnian government forces, which were engaged in a firefight with Bosnian Serb forces after a local cease-fire negotiated by UNPROFOR broke down (DOS).

August 13. American ABC television producer David Kaplan was killed by a sniper while traveling in a motorcade in Sarajevo with Prime Minister Milan Panic. He was hit in the back and died at the United Nations headquarters in Sarajevo (*New York Times*; DOS).

July. A CNN camerawoman was shot and severely wounded in July by sniper fire in Sarajevo. She is recovering after several operations at the Mayo Clinic in Rochester, Minnesota (*New York Times*).

May 18. An ICRC [International Committee of the Red Cross] convoy carrying food and medical relief was attacked as it entered Sarajevo, despite security guarantees obtained from the parties concerned. Three ICRC staff members were wounded and one of them, Frederic

APPENDIX I

Mauzice, died the next day in Sarajevo hospital (ICRC Bulletin No. 197).

April. A Belgian member of the [European Community] monitoring mission was killed south of Mostar, apparently in an attack by SDS forces (DOS).

MASS FORCIBLE EXPULSION
AND DEPORTATION OF CIVILIANS

November 2. A huge column of 15,000–30,000 Bosnians, mostly Muslims, thousands on foot, fled from Serbian assaults on Jajce and [from] three-way fighting between Serb, Croat, and Bosnian government forces in the area (DOS).

SIXTH REPORT
(MARCH 9, 1993)

WILLFUL KILLING

July–August 1992. A 20-year-old Bosnian Muslim from the village of Harambine, near Prijedor, described his capture by Serbian forces in July and the events leading to the murder of his father and five other men. He was held in Omarska camp for three weeks, from July 20 until August 6. During his time there, he witnessed the deaths of 20 men. . . . The witness fled his home on May

23, 1992, when Serbian soldiers attacked. . . . One hundred meters from the house, on the road leading to the center of Biscani, the soldiers stopped the group and searched them for valuables. Another 200 meters down the road, the group stopped again. This time the soldiers ordered the eight men, who lined up in pairs, to begin beating the man next to them in line. The witness was on the end of the line and standing next to his father, so he was being ordered to begin beating his father. Each of the pairs in the group were similar, with the father pitted against son, or brother versus brother.

After a short while, the man in the pair next to the witness refused the soldiers' exhortations to beat his son more fiercely. One of the soldiers then marched the man off the road and into the ditch, where he shot him.

By the end of the ordeal, six of the men either refused or were unable to continue beating their kin, and were executed. The witness and the youngest in the group managed to persuade the soldiers to spare them by lying and pleading that they were only 18 years old (DOS).

TORTURE OF PRISONERS

July 1992. A 15-year-old Bosnian Muslim girl from Kozarc described being gang-raped by at least eight Serbian soldiers and guards near Trnopolje. . . . Three days after her arrival at the prison, she went with a large number of women and other girls to fetch water from a well about 50 meters from the prison gates. [As they were] returning from the well, Trnopolje guards held back six girls, including the witness, and stopped them from reentering the prison gates. They were joined by four more female prisoners. Prison guards took the 10 girls to a house across the meadow. They were taken to the side yard of the house, out of sight of the roadway. Thirty Serbian soldiers, including "some dressed like a tank crew," were there and they taunted the girls, calling them "Turkish whores." The girls were ordered to undress or have their clothes pulled off. . . . A soldier approached the witness and mocked her, saying he had seen her before. Though she did not recognize him, he pulled out a photo of the witness with her 19-year-old Muslim boyfriend, whom he cursed for being in the Bosnian Territorial Defense Forces.

The man with the photograph raped her first. The witness said she fought and pulled his hair, but he bit her and hit her in the face. . . . Another rapist ran the blade of a knife across her breast as if to slice the skin off, leaving bleeding scratches. After that, she was raped eight more times before losing consciousness. When the witness regained consciousness, a Trnopolje guard who had attended her school came along and broke up the gang rape. As this guard and the witness headed back toward the gates of the Trnopolje camp, the witness said

APPENDIX I

the guard called back to the soldiers and the other guards, "Remember, you will be accountable for this!" (DOS).

ABUSE OF CIVILIANS IN DETENTION CENTERS

January 1993. A 23-year-old married Muslim female reported that she had been held through the first week of January with 600 women and girls in a gymnasium at the Doboj Middle School complex in north-central Bosnia. The witness and the other women were taken out in groups of 40 each day. Each woman was led to an individual classroom in the school and raped, then returned to the gymnasium. She said the guard told them they were being held for the purpose of "making Chetnik babies" (DOS).

IMPEDING DELIVERY OF FOOD AND MEDICAL SUPPLIES TO THE CIVILIAN POPULATION

February 20, 1993. Serbian forces in Borike halted a convoy of . . . trucks carrying emergency supplies to the Muslim community in Zepa (Reuters).

February 6, 1993. Serbian forces hit a German relief flight with antiaircraft fire. The C-160 was at 9,000 feet and just south of Karlovac when the antiaircraft fire hit near the right engine housing. The German loadmaster

APPENDIX I

was seriously wounded in the abdomen. U.N. peace-keeping troops witnessed the Serbs shooting at the German plane with 23-millimeter antiaircraft guns set up in Kosijersko Selo (DOS; *New York Times*; Reuters; Paris AFP; Bonn DDP).

DELIBERATE ATTACKS ON NONCOMBATANTS

February 18, 1993. Bosnian Serb gunners fired five tank shells from Sarajevo's Mrkovici Heights into the neurological surgery and pediatric surgery units of Kosevo Hospital. In addition, 20 shells damaged two other units in the hospital complex (Paris AFP).

February 11, 1993. Heavy shelling between Bosnian army and Serb troops caused the closing of the Sarajevo airport. The airlift operation from Zagreb was also suspended because British aircraft experienced two radar lock-ons. This shelling at the Sarajevo airport killed one French soldier and wounded three others (DOS; Paris AFP).

MASS FORCIBLE EXPULSION
AND DEPORTATION OF CIVILIANS

February 17, 1993. Bosnian Serbs showed Belgrade-based foreign journalists 35 bodies thus far exhumed from a grave site discovered the previous day near the

APPENDIX I

village of Kamenica, 20 kilometers south of Zvornik. The Serbs found two other grave sites, including one in a frozen pond containing 16 more bodies. . . . There had been a Muslim offensive in the area on November 6, 1992 (DOS; Paris AFP).

February 1993. By blocking relief supplies and general access, Serbian militia have starved Muslim refugees out of Cerska, Zvornik and Kamenica, forcing them to move to the Tuzla area of northern Bosnia. According to the U.N. spokeswoman on February 9: "They are horribly malnourished, they have severe frostbite and are showing signs of scabies, head lice, and war wounds. We have 50 severe cases of frostbite. Some of them are losing their fingers and their toes" (Paris AFP).

SUMMARY OF THE CIA REPORT TO THE SENATE INTELLIGENCE COMMITTEE AUGUST 9, 1995 ETHNIC CLEANSING AND ATROCITIES IN BOSNIA

Large-scale ethnic cleansing involving mass executions seemed to have subsided for much of 1993 and 1994. The capture of the U.N. "safe areas" in Srebrenica and Zepa in July 1995 saw its return on a massive scale, and for the first time Bosnian Serb leaders were directly

APPENDIX I

linked to the practice. The CIA released surveillance photos indicating the presence of mass graves around Srebrenica and suggested that electronic monitoring of Bosnian Serb communications indicated deliberate and organized involvement of Bosnian Serb army units. Reports of the wholesale executions of between 6,000 and 10,000 Bosnian Muslim men and boys from these two cities were confirmed by survivor testimony, U.N. sources, and independent news reports. CIA Deputy Director John Gannon in his testimony before the Senate Foreign Relations and Intelligence committees on August 9, 1995, concluded by asserting: "The apparently systematic, widespread nature of Serb actions strongly suggests [that], from the beginning of the conflict, Bosnian Serb political and military leaders have played a central role in the purposeful destruction and dispersal of Bosnia's non-Serb population."

PERSONS UNDER INDICTMENT

(For list of abbreviations see page 200)

As of November 16, 1995, twelve indictments naming fifty-two individuals have been issued by the war crimes tribunal. The Dayton Peace Accords require all the parties to assist the tribunal in bringing these individuals to justice. A list indicating the date of the indictment, the individuals named, and the crimes of which they are accused appears on the following pages:

APPENDIX I

11/04/94: SUSICA CAMP
Dragan Nikolic: g., v., c.

2/13/94: OMARSKA CAMP
Zeliko Meakic: g., v., gen., c.
Miroslav Kvoca: g., v., c.
Dragoljub Prcac: g., v., c.
Mladen Radic: g., v., c.
Milojica Kos: g., v., c.
Momcilo Gruban: g., v., c.
Zdravko Govedarica: g., v., c.
Gruban: g., v., c.
Predrag Kostic: g., v., c.
Nedeljko Paspalj: g., v., c.
Milan Pavlic: g., v., c.
Milutin Popovic: g., v., c.
Drazenko Predojevic: g., v., c.
Zeljko Savic: g., v., c.
Mirko Babic: g., v., c.
Nikica Janjic: g., v., c.
Dusan Knezevic: g., v., c.
Dragomir Saponja: g., v., c.
Zoran Zigic: g., v., c.

2/13/95: TADIC AND OTHER
Dusko Tadic: g., v., c.
Goran Borovinca: g., v., c.

7/21/95: KERATERM CAMP
Dusko Sikirica: g., v., gen., c.

APPENDIX I

Damir Dosen: g., v., c.
Dragan Fustar: g., v., c.
Dragan Kulundzija: g., v. c.
Nenad Banovic: g., v., c.
Predrag Banovic: g., v., c.
Goran Lajic: g., v., c.
Dragan Kondic: g., v., c.
Nikica Janic: g., v., c.
Dusan Knezvic: g., v., c.
Dragomir Saponja: g., v., c.
Zoran Zigic: g., v., c.
Nedeljko Timarac: g., v., c.
7/21/95: BOSANSKI SAMAC
Slobodan Miljkovic: g., v., gen., c.
Blagoje Simic: g., v., c.
Milan Simic: g., c.
Miroslav Tadic: g., c.
Steven Todorovic: g., v., c.
Simo Zaric: g., c.
7/21/95: BRCKO
Goran Jelisic: g., v., gen., c.
Ranko Cesic: g., v., c.
7/25/95: MARTIC
Milan Martic
7/25/95: KARADZIC and MLADIC
Radovan Karadzic: g., v., gen., c.
Ratko Mladic: g., v., gen., c.

APPENDIX I

8/25/95:   STUPNI DO
           Ivica Rajic: g., v.

7/11/95:   VUKOVAR HOSPITAL
           Milan Mrksic: g., v., c.
           Miroslav Radic: g., v., c.
           Veselin Sljivancanin: g., v., c.

11/10/95:   LASVA VALLEY
           Dario Koric: g., v., c.
           Tihofil Blaskic: g., v., c.
           Mario Cerkez: g., v., c.
           Ivan Santic: g., v., c.
           Pero Skopljak: g., v., c.
           Zlatko Aleksovski: g., v., c.

11/16/95:   SREBINICA
           Radovan Karadzic: v., gen., v.
           Ratko Mladic: v., gen., v.

Abbreviations

g: Grave breaches of the 1949 Geneva Conventions
v: Violations of the laws and customs of war
gen: Genocide
c: Crimes against humanity

MILITARY
ASSETS
OF THE
BALKAN STATES

The following information was derived from the 1994–95, 1993–1994, and 1992–93 editions of *The Military Balance*, produced by the International Institute for Strategic Studies, London, and used with permission of The Oxford University Press. The information is supplied to provide a concise reference source of the combat power of each of the Balkan states. For additional details on the type and number of these and other combat systems, together with the limitations of these data, the reader is directed to those references for specific information. It should be understood that no attempt has been made by the author to assess the readiness or the operational capabilities of any of the nations' military forces or particular units. This information is not intended to be used for operational planning.

APPENDIX II

Abbreviations

Est.: ....Estimated
Helo.: ....Helicopter
Hvy Mrts: ....Heavy mortars
Mult. Rk Lch.: ....Multiple Rocket Launchers
Paramilitary: ......Includes border guards, police, internal security forces
Self Prp: ....Self-propelled artillery
Towed: ....Towed artillery pieces

APPENDIX II

ALBANIA

TOTAL ARMED FORCES:
Active: 73,000
Reserves: 155,000
Paramilitary: 13,500

WEAPONS SYSTEMS:

Army
Main Battle Tanks: 859
　　　　　T-34, T-54/59, T-62

Artillery: 633
　　　　　Assorted 122mm, 130mm, 152mm of Chinese
　　　　　manufacture
　　　　　Mult. Rk Lch: 270, 107mm
　　　　　Hvy Mrts: 759

Navy
Submarines: 2
　　　　　Soviet Whiskey class

Surface Combatants: 0

Patrol Craft: 35

APPENDIX II

Air Force

Combat Aircraft: 99

Assorted J-2, J-4, J-6, J-7 models (Chinese variants of MiG-15, MiG-17F, MiG-19, MiG-21 aircraft)

No Combat Helo.

APPENDIX II

BOSNIA-HERZEGOVINA

TOTAL ARMED FORCES:
Est. 110,000

WEAPONS SYSTEMS:

Army
Main Battle Tanks: Est. 40
T-34, T-55s assorted operational levels

Artillery: unknown numbers of 130mm, 203mm.
Mult. Rk Lch: 40+
Hvy Mrts: 300

Navy
None

Air Force
None

APPENDIX II

BULGARIA

TOTAL ARMED FORCES:

Active: 101,900

Reserves: 303,000

Paramilitary: 12,000

WEAPONS SYSTEMS:

Army

Main Battle Tanks: 1,967

358 T-34, 1,276 T-55, 333 T-72

Artillery: 2,053
Towed: 731
Self Prp: 656
Mult. Rk Lch: 222
Hvy Mrts: 444

Navy

Submarines : 2

Soviet Romeo class

Surface Combatants: 1 Frigate

Patrol Craft: 21

APPENDIX II

Air Force

Combat Aircraft: 294

Assorted MiG-21, Mi-G 23, MiG 29, and Su-25

Combat Helo.: 44

Assorted Mi-2, Mi-8/17, Mi-24

APPENDIX II

CROATIA

TOTAL ARMED FORCES:

Active: Est. 105,000

Reserve: 180,000

Paramilitary: 40,000

ETHNIC CROATIAN FORCES OPERATING IN BOSNIA:
Est. 50,000. Note: these forces possess their own weapons and as of December 1995 were working in conjunction with Bosnian government forces.

WEAPONS SYSTEMS:

Army

Main Battle Tanks: 344
　　　　　　　　Assorted T-34, T-54, T-84

Artillery: Est. 900
　　　　　Towed: Assorted 76mm, 85mm, 100mm, 105mm, 130mm, 152mm and 203mm
　　　　　Self Prp: 2
　　　　　Mult. Rk Lch: Assort. unknown number
　　　　　Hvy Mrts: Assort. unknown number

APPENDIX II

Navy

Submarines: 1

Una class

Surface Combatants: None

Patrol Craft: 9

Air Force

Combat Aircraft: 300

Including 2 MiG 21

Combat Helo.: 15

Mi-8 attack helicopters

APPENDIX II

GREECE

TOTAL ARMED FORCES:

Active: 159,300

Reserves: 406,000

Paramilitary: 26,500

WEAPONS SYSTEMS:

Army

Main Battle Tanks: 2,722

396 M-47, (in storage) 1,220 M-48, 671 M-60, 156 AMX-30 (in storage), 279 Leopard

Artillery: 2,709
Towed: 875
Self Prp: 371
Hvy Mrts: 1,463

Navy

Submarines: 8

8 Ge-T -209/1100

APPENDIX II

Surface Combatants: 14

6 Destroyers (Assorted), 8 Frigates

Patrol Craft: 42

Air Force

Combat Aircraft: 788 (102 in storage)

Assorted A-7, F-4, F-5, F-16, F-104;
Mirage F-1, Mirage 2000

Combat Helo.: None

APPENDIX II

HUNGARY

TOTAL ARMED FORCES:

Active: 74,500

Reserves: 195,000

Paramilitary: 730

WEAPONS SYSTEMS:

Army

Main Battle Tanks: 1,191 (323 in storage)
5 T-34, 34 T-54, 1,014 T-55, 138 T-72

Artillery: 991
Towed: 566
Self Prp: 151
Mult. Rk. Lch: 56
Hvy Mrts: 218

Navy
None

APPENDIX II

Air Force

Combat Aircraft: 171

Assorted MiG-21,23,29 Su-22

Combat Helo.: None

APPENDIX II

MACEDONIA

TOTAL ARMED FORCES:
 Active: 10,400
 Reserves: 100,000 (Planned)
 Paramilitary: 7,500

WEAPONS SYSTEMS:

Army
Several T-34's

Navy
None

Air Force
Forming, planning for 50 Helicopters
No Combat Aircraft

APPENDIX II

ROMANIA

TOTAL ARMED FORCES:

Active: 203,500

Reserves: 427,000

Paramilitary: 23,800

WEAPONS SYSTEMS:

Army

Main Battle Tanks: 2,394
686 T-34, 822 T-55, 30 T-72, 632 TR-85, 224 TR-580

Artillery: 3,138
Towed: 1,412
Self Prp: 48
Mult. Rk Lch: 384
Hvy Mrts: 1,294

Navy

Submarines: 1
Soviet Kilo class

APPENDIX II

Surface Combatants: 6

1 Destroyer, 5 Frigates

Patrol Craft: 82

Air Force

Combat Aircraft: 382

Assorted MiG 15, 17, 21, 23, 29, IAR-93

Combat Helo.: 179

Assorted IAR-316B, IAR-330-H, Mi-8, Mi-17, SA-365N

APPENDIX II

SERBIA/MONTENEGRO

TOTAL ARMED FORCES:

Active: 126,500

Reserves: 400,000

Ethnic Serbian Forces operating in Bosnia, Est. 80,000

Ethnic Serbian Forces operating in Croatia, Est. 40,000–50,000 prior to expulsion in August 1995. Note: these forces possessed their own weapons.

Paramilitary: Unknown

WEAPONS SYSTEMS:

Army

Main Battle Tanks: 639
          407 T-54, 232 M-84

Artillery: Est. 1,489
          Towed: 786
          Self Prp: Est. 75
          Mult Rk Lch: 72
          Hvy Mtrs: 556

APPENDIX II

Navy

Most of the former Yugoslav naval bases are in Croatian hands, and some of the following assets may now be under Croatian control.

Submarines: 5
> 2 Sava and 3 Herj class

Surface Combatants: 4
> Frigates

Patrol Craft.: 40

Air Force

Combat Aircraft: 284
> Assorted P-2 Kraguj, Jastreb, Super Galeb, MiG-21, 29

Combat Helo.: 115
> Assorted Mi-8, Gazela (attack)

APPENDIX II

SLOVENIA

TOTAL ARMED FORCES:

Active: 8,100

Reserves: Est. 70,000

Paramilitary: 4,500 (plus 5,000 reserve)

WEAPONS SYSTEMS:

Army
Main Battle Tanks: 57

Assorted M-84, T-55

Artillery: 45 (Mortars)

Navy
None

Air Force
100 Combat Helo. Gazelle

APPENDIX II

TURKEY

TOTAL ARMED FORCES:

Active: 503,800

Reserves: 952,300

Paramilitary: 70,000 (plus 50,000 reserves)

WEAPONS SYSTEMS:

Army

Main Battle Tanks: 4,919 (586 in storage)
Assorted M-47, M-48, Leopard.

Artillery: 4,275
Towed: 1,576
Self Prp: 821
Mult. Rk Lch: 35
Hvy Mrts:1,843

Navy

Submarines: 15
Assorted U.S. Guppy, Tang, and Ge Type
209/1200

APPENDIX II

Surface Combatants: 21

5 Destroyers, 16 Frigates

Patrol Craft: 45

Air Force

Combat Aircraft: 710 (122 in storage)

Assorted F-4, F-5, F-16, F-104, S-2A-Tracker

Combat Helo.: 21

U.S. Uh-1H

BIBLIOGRAPHY

BOOKS

Asprey, Robert B. *War in the Shadows: The Guerrilla in History*. Book Club Ed., Vol. I, Garden City, N.Y.: Doubleday, 1975.

Carnegie Endowment for International Peace. *The Other Balkan Wars*. Washington, D.C.: Brookings Institution Publications, 1993.

Center for Strategic and International Studies. *The Military Balance: 1992–93*. New York: Macmillan, 1992.

Center for Strategic and International Studies. *The Mil-

BIBLIOGRAPHY

itary Balance: 1993–94. London: Brassey's, 1993.

Center for Strategic and International Studies. *The Military Balance: 1994–95*. London: Brassey's, 1993.

Cigar, Norman. *Genocide in Bosnia*. College Station: Texas A&M University Press, 1995.

Europa Publications Ltd. *The Europa World Year Book: 1994*. Rochester, England: Europa Publications, 1994.

Europa Publications Ltd. *The Europa World Year Book: 1995*. Rochester, England: Europa Publications, 1995.

Glenny, Misha. *The Fall of Yugoslavia*. New York: Penguin, 1992.

Kaplan, Robert D. *Balkan Ghosts: A Journey through History*. New York: St. Martin's Press, 1993.

Schevill, Ferdinand. *The History of the Balkan Peninsula: From the Earliest Times to the Present Day*. New York: Harcourt Brace, 1922.

Singleton, Fred. *Twentieth-Century Yugoslavia*. Great Britain: Macmillan, 1976.

Stankovic, Slobadan. *The End of the Tito Era: Yugoslavia's Dilemmas*. Stanford, Calif.: Hoover Institution Press, 1981.

Thompson, Mark. *A Paper House: The Ending of Yugoslavia*. New York: Pantheon Books, 1992.

Tuchman, Barbara W. *The Guns of August*. New York: Macmillan, 1962.

BIBLIOGRAPHY

ENCYCLOPEDIAS

"The Balkans," *Colliers Encyclopedia*, 1992, Vol. 3, p. 438.

"Greece," *The New Encyclopedia Britannica*, 1987, Vol. 20, p. 363.

"Tito," *Colliers Encyclopedia*, 1992, Vol. 22, p. 338.

"Turkey," *The New Encyclopedia Britannica*, 1987, Vol. 28, p. 890.

"Yugoslavia," *The New Encyclopedia Britannica*, 1987, Vol. 29, p. 1043.

ARTICLES

Bassiouni, M. Cherif, and Thomas Dimitroff, "Peace without Justice," *Transitions*, Nov. 3, 1995, p. 13.

Bell-Fialfoff, Andrew, "A Brief History of Ethnic Cleansing," *Foreign Affairs*, Summer 1993, p. 110.

Brzezinski, Zbigniew, "Fifty Years after Yalta, A New Chance for Europe and the Balkans," *Transitions*, May 12, 1995, p. 40.

Carbaravic, Zltan, "An Escalating Power Struggle over Bosnia's Political Future," *Transitions*, Nov. 3, 1995, p. 22.

Donia, Robert, "A Test Case for the Muslim-Croat Federation," *Transitions*, Nov. 3, 1995, p. 24.

Erik, Norman, "Croatia's Special Police," *Jane's Intelligence Review*, Vol. 7, No. 7, p. 291.

BIBLIOGRAPHY

Fatic, Aleksandar, "Tudjman Takes the Offensive," *Transitions*, May 12, 1995, p. 36.

Gallager, Tom, "Bosnian Brotherhood," *Transitions*, Mar. 15, 1995, p. 23.

Glyn-Pickett, Julie, "A Last Bastion of Ethnic Tolerance," *Transitions*, Nov. 3, 1995, p. 18.

Gow, James, "Settling Bosnia—The Balance of Forces," *Jane's Intelligence Review*, April 1994, p. 174.

Hoffman, Frank, "Where Will All These People Go," *Transitions*, Nov. 3, 1995, p. 19.

Huntington, Samuel P., "The Clash of Civilizations," *Foreign Affairs*, Summer 1993, p. 22.

Ivanovic, Miodrag, "The Fate of the Yugoslav Military Industry," *Jane's Intelligence Review*, March 1993, p. 164.

———, "The M-84 ABI—Implications for Tank Production in the Former Yugoslavia," *Jane's Intelligence Review*, Vol. 7, No. 5, p. 205.

Jordan, Michael, "Rape as Warfare," *Transitions*, Nov. 3, 1995, p. 21.

Karadzic, Rodoban, Speech Experts "Milosevic as Traitor," *Transitions*, Sept. 8, 1995, p. 53.

King, Colin, "Former Yugoslavia—Land Mines," *Jane's Intelligence Review*, Vol. 7, No. 1, p. 15.

Kjilas, Aleksa, "A Profile of Slobodan Milosevic," *Foreign Affairs*, Summer 1993, p. 122.

Kramer, Diedrick, "Dutch Peacekeepers under Fire in

BIBLIOGRAPHY

the Aftermath of Srebrenica," *Transitions*, Nov. 1995, p. 16.

Markovitch, Stan, "Milosevic Flexes His Political Muscle," *Transitions*, Jan. 30, 1995, p. 55.

———, "Milosevic's Renewed Attack on the Independent Media," *Transitions*, Jan. 30, 1995, p. 26.

———, "Stable Support for Extremism?," *Transitions*, March 29, 1995, p. 31.

———, "Milosevic Backtracks," *Transitions*, Apr. 11, 1995, p. 66.

———, "A Potent Weapon in Milosevic's Arsenal," *Transitions*, April 28, 1995, p. 35.

———, "Opposition Parties Attempt Unity—Again," *Transitions*, June 9, 1995, p. 20.

———, "New Image, Same Old Goals," *Transitions*, July 14, 1995, p. 6.

———, "Milosevic's New Strategy," *Transitions*, Oct. 20, 1995, p. 60.

Marx, Stefan, "Reforms under the Double-Headed Eagle," *Jane's Intelligence Review*, September 1994, p. 392.

Matic, Veran, "The Rump Yugoslavia as the New Balkan 'Black Hole,' " *Transitions*, Oct. 6, 1995, p. 34.

Meron, Theodore, "The Case for War Crimes Trials in Yugoslavia," *Foreign Affairs*, Summer 1993, p. 122.

Mickey, Robert W., "Unstable in a Stable Way," *Transitions*, Jan. 30, 1995, p. 38.

BIBLIOGRAPHY

Milivojevic, Marko, "Croatia's Intelligence Service," *Jane's Intelligence Review*, September 1994, p. 404.

———, "The 'Balkan Medellin,' " *Jane's Intelligence Review*, Vol. 7, No. 2, p. 68.

———, "Slovenia—An Arms Bazaar," *Jane's Intelligence Review*, November 1994, p. 496.

Moore, Patrick, "Dashed Hopes, Endless Conflict," *Transitions*, Jan. 30, 1995, p. 20.

———, "January in Bosnia: Bizarre Diplomacy," *Transitions*, March 15, 1995, p. 20.

———, "The Winds of War Return," *Transitions*, April 14, 1995, p. 32.

———, "Waiting and Watching in the Wake of Western Slavonia," *Transitions*, June 23, 1995, p. 28.

———, "Karadzic Takes the International Community Hostage," *Transitions*, July 14, 1995, p. 2.

———, "An End Game in Croatia and Bosnia," *Transitions*, Nov. 3, 1995, p. 6.

———, "Milosevic's War: The Tide Turns," *Transitions*, Nov. 3, 1995, p. 4.

Moyland, Suzanne von, "Macedonia—Home But Not Yet Dry," *Jane's Intelligence Review*, Vol. 2, No. 2, p. 64.

Parrish, Scott, "Twisting in the Wind: Russia and the Yugoslav Conflict," *Transitions*, Nov. 3, 1995, p. 28.

Perry, Duncan, "On the Road to Stability—Or Destruction?" *Transitions*, Aug. 25, 1995, p. 40.

BIBLIOGRAPHY

Pfaff, William, "Invitation to War," *Foreign Affairs*, Summer 1993, p. 97.

Ripley, Tim, "Croatia's Strategic Situation," *Jane's Intelligence Review*, Vol. 7, No. 1, p. 29.

Schmidt, Fabian, "Between Political Strife and a Developing Economy," *Transitions*, Jan. 30, 1995, p. 8.

———, "From National Consensus to Pluralism," *Transitions*, March 29, 1995, p. 26.

———, "Balancing the Power Triangle," *Transitions*, May 26, 1995, p. 34.

———, "Winning Wary Recognition for Democratic Reforms," *Transitions*, Aug. 25, 1995, p. 3.

———, "Strategic Reconciliation in Kosovo," *Transitions*, Aug. 25, 1995, p. 17.

———, "Show Trials in Kosovo," *Transitions*, Nov. 3, 1995, p. 36.

Shafir, Michael, "The 'Centripetfugal' Process of Unifying the Liberals," *Transitions*, Aug. 25, 1995, p. 70.

Sullivan, Marianne, "Seeking the Security of Military Might," *Transitions*, Aug. 25, 1995, p. 8.

———, "Mending Relations with Greece," *Transitions*, Aug. 25, 1995, p. 11.

Urban, Jan, "Sarajevo to NATO: Jet'aime," *Transitions*, Nov. 3, 1995, p. 27.

Vasic-Janekovic, Jane, "Trials of a War Tribunal," *Transitions*, Nov. 3, 1995, p. 11.

Vego, Milan, "The Army of Bosnia and Herzegovina,"

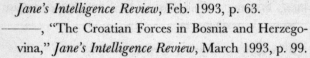

Jane's Intelligence Review, Feb. 1993, p. 63.

———, "The Croatian Forces in Bosnia and Herzegovina," *Jane's Intelligence Review*, March 1993, p. 99.

———, "The Croatian Army," *Jane's Intelligence Review*, May 1993, p. 203.

———, "The Yugoslav Ground Forces," *Jane's Intelligence Review*, July 1993, p. 247.

———, "The Muslim Defense Industry in Bosnia and Herzegovina," *Jane's Intelligence Review*, May 1994, p. 213.

———, "The New Yugoslav Air and Air Defense Forces," *Jane's Intelligence Review*, July 1994, p. 297.

Wolfowitz, Paul, "They Must Be Equipped to Defend Themselves," *Wall Street Journal*, December 12, 1995.

Wohlstetter, Albert, "Why We're in It—Still," *Wall Street Journal*, July 1, 1993, p. A14.

———, "The Way Out," *Wall Street Journal*, July 2, 1993, p. A6.

———, "Since Bosnia Has Been Reduced to This . . . ," *Wall Street Journal*, December 12, 1995.

Xhudo, Gus, "The Balkan Albanians—Biding Their Time?," *Jane's Intelligence Review*, Vol. 7, No. 5, p. 208.

Zanga, Louis, "Corruption Takes Its Toll on the Berisha Government," *Transitions*, May 12, 1995, p. 12.

BIBLIOGRAPHY

Zoran, Solomun, "All I Want Is for Ethnic Cleansing to Stop," *Transitions*, Nov. 3, 1995, p. 35.

GOVERNMENT PUBLICATIONS

Center for Military History, *The German Antiguerrilla Operations in the Balkans (1941–1944)*, U.S. Army, (Fac. Ed., 1989).

———, *The German Campaigns in the Balkans (Spring 1941)*, U.S. Army, (Fac. Ed. 1984, 1986).

Central Intelligence Agency, *Eastern Europe*, Atlas, (Gov. Print. Off.), 1990.

———, *The Former Yugoslavia*, Atlas, (Gov. Print. Off.) 1992.

———, *World Factbook 1992*, (Gov. Print. Off.) 1992.

———, *World Factbook 1993*, (Gov. Print. Off.) 1993.

———, *World Factbook 1994*, (Gov. Print. Off.) 1994.

———, *World Factbook 1995*, (Gov. Print. Off.) 1995.

———, "Ethnic Cleansing and Atrocities in Bosnia," Statement by Deputy Director for Intelligence John Gannon, before the Joint Hearings of the Senate Select Committee on Intelligence and the Senate Foreign Relations Committee, August 9, 1995.

CRS Report for Congress, "Serbia, Montenegro (Federal Republic of Yugoslavia) Background and Current Issues," January 11, 1993, (Julie Kim, analyst).

———, "Bosnia-Herzegovina: Background to the Conflict," January 21, 1993 (Steven J. Woeherl, analyst).

BIBLIOGRAPHY

————, "Bosnia: U.S. Objectives, Military Options, Serbian Responses," April 14, 1993 (Mark M. Lowenthal, analyst).

————, "Yugoslavia Crisis and U.S. Policy," August 13, 1993, (Steven J. Woehrel and Julie Kim, analysts).

————, "Bosnia and Macedonia: U.S. Military Operations," December 1, 1995 (Steven R. Bowman, analyst).

————, "Bosnia—Former Yugoslavia: Ongoing Conflict and U.S. Policy," December 1, 1995 (Steven Woehrel and Julie Kim, analysts).

Department of Defense, *The Former Yugoslavia Handbook*, 1993.

————, "On the Deployment of U.S. Troops with the Bosnia Peace Implementation Force," Statement of Secretary of Defense William J. Perry before the Senate Committee on Foreign Relations, December 1, 1995.

————, *The Dayton Peace Accords*, Official Text. BosniaLink: http://www.dtic.dla.mil/bosnia

Foreign Broadcast Information Service, "Speech by Slobodan Milosevic, President Serbian LC Central Committee Presidium, April 25, 1987 (April 27, 1993).

Joint Public Research Service, *Suppressed Memorandum of Members of Serbian Academy of Science and Art*, JPRS DOC. 92BA1158A September 1986.

To Stand against Aggression: Milosevic, The Bosnian

BIBLIOGRAPHY

Republic, and the Conscience of the West, Senator Joseph Biden, 103rd Cong. 1st Sess. (April 1993).

United Nations, *Final Report of the Commission of Experts Established Pursuant to Security Council Resolution 780*, U.N. Document #S/1994/674.

U.S. Government, *American Policy in Bosnia*, Hearing before the Subcommittee on European Affairs of the Senate Committee on Foreign Relations, 103 Cong. 1st Sess. (February 18, 1993).

Arthur L. Clark has a B.A. in history from Marquette University, and a J.D. and M.A. in International Affairs from Catholic University. He graduated with distinction from the U.S. Naval War College and has served as a research assistant in the Executive Office of the President, Office of National Drug Control Policy. He is a Major in the U.S. Marine Corps Reserve.